NEGRO SCULPTURE

CARL EINSTEIN

NEGRO SCULPTURE

**TRANSLATED
BY PATRICK HEALY**

INCLUDING ALL ORIGINAL PLATES

NOVEMBER EDITIONS
MMXVI

© 2016 November Editions / Patrick Healy

First published in ebook format in 2014

This translation is based on the first edition of *Negerplastik*, published in 1915 by the Weissen Bücher Verlag in Leipzig.

Author portrait drawn by Ludwig Meidner, 1913.

Design and layout: The Curved House

All rights reserved. This book or any portion thereof may not be reproduced or used in any manner whatsoever without the express written permission of the publisher, except for the use of brief quotations in a book review.

ISBN 978-94-92027-10-8

November Editions – Amsterdam

For inquiries please contact us at hello@novembereditions.com

www.NovemberEditions.com

CONTENTS

INTRODUCTION 1

NEGRO SCULPTURE

REMARKS ON METHOD 11

THE PAINTERLY 16

RELIGION AND AFRICAN ART 21

THREE-DIMENSIONAL SPATIAL VISION 26

MASKS AND RELATED PRACTICES 37

PLATES 41

INTRODUCTION

Carl Einstein (1885-1940) has been called the 'prophet of the avant-garde'[1]. He was born in the town of Neuwied and, after a childhood spent in Karlsruhe, moved to Berlin in 1904 to study art history and philosophy, attending lectures by Heinrich Wölfflin and Georg Simmel amongst others. During this time he befriended Gottfried Benn, and began frequenting the Café des Westens (also known by its nickname 'Café Grossenwahn' or 'Megalomania'), the meeting point of a wide array of artists and writers such as George Grosz, Rudolf Belling, Else Lasker-Schüler and Franz Pfemfert.

Einstein quickly established himself as an author and art critic of renown. In 1907, Franz Blei's *Die Opale* published the first instalments of his experimental anti- or metanovel *Bebuquin*. This work, a crucial early example of literary Expressionism, would subsequently be serialised in its entirety in Franz Pfemfert's *Die Aktion* in 1912 and finally be published in book form by Pfemfert's press of the same name later that year.

In 1915 Einstein voluntarily joined the army and was stationed in Brussels. After the war he returned to Berlin and resumed his writing life, publishing in a variety of journals and magazines such as *Die Pleite* and *Das Kunstblatt* and editing a satirical paper called *Der blutige Ernst*. However, confronted with the rise of the Nazi party, who regarded him as a communist, Einstein eventually decided to leave Berlin for Paris in 1928. Here, he worked with Georges Bataille to cofound the magazine *Documents*[2] and with Eugene Jolas, who would publish a chapter of *Bebuquin* in his own journal, *transition* (which also featured the work of writers such as Benn, Beckett and Joyce).

In 1936, Einstein volunteered as a soldier in the Spanish civil war, fighting on the side of the anarchist Durruti column. He returned to Paris in 1937; three years later he would be arrested by the Vichy government and incarcerated in a concentration camp in the Pyrenees. Upon his release, Einstein, a Jew and anti-fascist, found himself trapped between the advancing Nazi troops and the border of Franco's Spain. Seeing no other option, he took his own life on July 5 1940 by jumping into the river at the town of Lestelle-Bétharram.

Einstein's *Negerplastik*, the *editio princeps* of which appeared in 1915 with the Weissen Bücher Verlag in Leipzig, is considered to be the first account of African art, specifically sculpture, to challenge various prejudices and misconceptions around this subject, by a European critic.[3] Many features of the publication struck contemporary reviewers as unusual.[4] One of the most commented on was that the book as issued by the publishers contained over 100 plates, none of which had captions or identifications.[5] In the body of the text Einstein only refers to the fact of dated Benin sculpture and nowhere to a specific work, other than mentioning towards the end the different kinds of masks he is referring to, but again in a very generic way. Moreover, there is no discussion of how his analysis of the working of sculptures can be communicated by photographs in black and white, nor any reference to ethnographic or other writing on or from Africa.

Remarkably, Einstein followed up the second edition of *Negerplastik* with an independent book publication entitled *Afrikanische Plastik*,[6] where the text is much more forthright about his aims and methods and also spells out the complexities of giving an account of African art. It is clear that he sees his own work as a new beginning in this respect. In 1925, finally, Einstein edited a collection of African legends, and it is here that one finds some of the texts which he must have been studying earlier on.[7]

The dense and complex text of *Negerplastik* remains one of the most striking interventions of Einstein's working life as a writer and leading catalyst of modernism, and indispensable for the understanding of the shift in discussion towards non-European art works that occurred at this time. It is one of the main aims of the work to establish that African sculpture has independent achievement as art, and cannot be understood by the system of sculptural production developed by the Europeans. Further in the text, Einstein refutes what had become the dominant arguments around sculpture and the viewing experience in the West, especially as argued in the work of Adolf von Hildebrand, *The Problem of Form*, which made such a significant impact from the time of its first appearance in 1893.[8]

Einstein creates an aesthetic theory which challenges on the face of it the dominant development in German academic life since the time of the publication of Kant's *Critique of the Power of Judgement*, and specifically its technical development in the works of Hildebrand and Heinrich Wölfflin, resulting in what many considered as the proper scientific working out of the principles of art history and the basis for further works with a claim to being sculpture. As Conor Joyce has shown, Einstein directly used his reflections on African art to create an absolute category called *das Plastische*, 'the sculptural'.[9] This category formed an emphatic and powerful conceptual challenge to previous theories, because Einstein was to argue that there is an immediate grasp of form in the perception of a sculpture and that what is expressed is three-dimensional space. For Einstein sculpture and space are identical.

The first and main point is to grasp that in challenging the theory of Hildebrand, Einstein is arguing for a different way of seeing and viewing African art. What resonates throughout *Negerplastik*, and is often repeated, is that the European engagement has been hindered in many ways, but mostly in the failure to understand the creation of a new object and the formal achievement of African art work. European awareness is fatally flawed by virtue of prejudice and an overweening sense of superiority, a master narrative of the development of art which is exclusionary of other cultures and productions. Moreover, there is the ethnographic fantasy of origins and the ascription of the notion of 'primitive' as a dominant explanatory category.

In his later *Afrikanische Plastik* Einstein emphasises again and again how difficult the task of saying something meaningful about African sculpture is. What he takes as the correct starting point is the sculpture itself and the sculptural experience, which is the experience of the absolute, self-enclosed and independent unity of the work; not the emphasis on frontality, silhouette and viewpoint stressed by Hildebrand and Konrad Fiedler for the visual appreciation of the effect of three-dimensional work.[10]

Einstein will engage in formal analysis, and this will demonstrate that African sculpture is art in any meaningful sense. He stresses that the individual creation is not just a product of personal force, but exists in a field of forces religious, moral and social, which become concrete and singular in the work. By unpacking also the aesthetic presuppositions of European sculpture, for example the emphasis on frontality (which Einstein takes not to be the primitive aspect of form but as a pictorial anticipation of volume), he points to the diminishing of 'plastic vision' in the Western tradition. For Einstein the development of the blending of the sculptural and the pictorial since the Baroque has led inevitably to impressionism and pictorial means, and he notes that in his own time it is painters, and not sculptors, who have pursued the question of the three dimensional. Although he is not named directly, it is clearly Cézanne who is the outstanding instance here.[11]

The blending of the pictorial and sculptural, with its consequent destruction of the plastic, also has an analogy by instantiation in the relation of the viewer and the work. The viewer, Einstein adds, is integrated into the work and becomes an indispensable function, with the sculptor creating the 'other' of the viewer to multiply the means and effects to communicate. Spatial construction is sacrificed and three-dimensional space forgotten in this specular alterity of seeking communicable effects. The crisis in the contemporary situation of sculpture is most completely visible in France. The French painters however did see what had to be remedied, and this brought about the recognition of the pure sculptural form that African art, even in isolation, had created. As Einstein will argue, abstraction is the wrong term for this achievement; rather, through the direct grasping of space African sculpture will prove in the most formal sense a powerful realism.

Einstein makes the unequivocal statement that African art is above all else determined by religion. The distantial work offered to the divine is set away from its maker; it is an act of religious devotion. The work is created in worship and terror; it is the divine, and thus necessarily separate and full of the pathos of distance, autonomous and ultimately self-contained. The work totally removed from the viewer must be a total space and not fragmentary. Here Einstein locates the first and most compelling rebuttal to then-current theories of sculpture.

It is the perfection of the form, even the strengthening of the autonomous parts, which this religious situation brings about; through its very intensity it is developed to the point of being fully self-enclosed. Finite, closed form and religion correspond with each other, since the art work is a mystical reality and unity, and not a symbol. The god keeps enclosed the mythical reality. The unity of perception of the work which Hildebrand sought to explain is made redundant in this account. Here in the divine there is no becoming, the work absorbs the space of three dimensions and becomes atemporal.

Having argued this vivid religious reality, Einstein returns to account for the three-dimensional spatial vision, the cubic apprehension. The three dimensions must not be given via the optical, but rather directly, as complete and real expression. Step by step Einstein dismantles Hildebrand's schema, based on frontality and the silhouette, and posits the need to understand the three-dimensional as integrated into a single visual field through the concatenation of forces which in African art, paradoxically, is found via the formal dimension. Art is unconditioned intensity and the quality of the integration of form in plastic vision. It is this clarification of form which achieves the autonomy of the work.

What is clear is that Einstein is driving his arguments towards an inexorable conclusion, namely that African sculpture is the only pure sculpture there is. The section on three-dimensional spatial vision forms the densest and most precise part of the text; although short, it requires careful reading to follow the full weight of Einstein's revolt against the dominant figures of Hildebrand and Wölfflin. No writer on African art before Einstein had ever struggled with such respect and understanding to give an account and none were so aware of the limitations, or so decisive in the rich and full appraisal of the art of African sculpture. In the robust articulation of modernism of which Einstein was a pivotal figure, the text is still striking in its boldness and the originality of its aesthetic view; it is also indispensable for understanding the full development of Einstein's thinking about art, which was to culminate in his 1926 *Die Kunst des 20. Jahrhunderts*,[12] a work that in the awful development of politics and power in Germany was to become the handbook for those who set out to destroy the extraordinary achievements of the modern revolution in the arts.

NOTES

1. *Carl Einstein. Prophet der Avantgarde*, ed. Klaus Siebenhaar (Berlin: Fannei & Walz Verlag, 1991). For Einstein's impact on advanced tendencies in artistic modernism also see Rolf-Peter Baacke in the essay "Carl-Einstein – Kunstagent", in his *Carl Einstein, Materialien*, Vol.1 (Berlin: Silver und Goldstein, 1990), pp. 9-27.

2. For Einstein's work with Bataille see Conor Joyce, *Carl Einstein in Documents, and his collaboration with Georges Bataille* (Philadelphia: XLibris, 2003).

3. For details of the publication and reviews see the Rolf-Peter Baacke volume given in note 1 above. Readers might also consult the special issue of *October*, 107, and the contribution of Sebastian Zeidler to Jean-Maurice Monnoyer's *Walter Benjamin, Carl Einstein et les arts primitifs* (University of Pau, 1999) has a fascinating and extended discussion on the question of the photographic reproduction of such works.

4. These reviews and other contemporary documents are contained in Rolf-Peter Baacke, pp. 83-120, see note 1 above. Details concerning Einstein's Paris contacts with critics and dealers are given by Hans Purrmann. Hermann Hesse reviews *Negerplastik* as 'completely philosophical' and notes the deliberate lack of specific detail.

5. The identification of the plates has been undertaken by Ezio Bassani and Jean-Louis Paudrat. For this list and discussion see Lilliane Meffre, *La sculpture nègre* (Paris: L'Harmattan, 1998).

6. Carl Einstein, *Afrikanische Plastik* (Berlin: Wasmuth Verlag, 1921), in which the plates are listed and bibliography is given at pp.33-4. Helpful in reconstructing Einstein's sources.

7. *Afrikanische Märchen und Legenden*, ed. by Carl Einstein (Berlin: Rowohlt, 1925).

8. Adolf von Hildebrand, *Das Problem der Form in der bildenden Kunst* (Strasbourg, 1893).

9. Conor Joyce, *Carl Einstein in Documents*. Especially Appendix IV. See note 2 above.

10. The most complete discussion of Fiedler can be found in *Empathy, Form and Space: Problems in German Aesthetics*, ed. by H. F. Mallgrave and E. Ikonomou (Santa Monica: Getty Center, 1994).

11. For a slightly earlier analysis of the painterly implications of such research and particularly Cézanne, see Max Raphael, *Von Monet zu Picasso* (Munich: Delphin Verlag, 1913).

12. *Die Kunst des 20. Jahrhunderts* (Berlin: Propyläen, 1931).

NEGRO SCULPTURE

REMARKS ON METHOD

There is hardly any other art which Europeans approach with so much mistrust as African art. The first move is to even deny that there is such a thing as 'art', and then to emphasise the distance which separates such products from the creations of the Europeans, with a contempt that leads to demeaning terminology. Such distance, and the prejudices which flow from it, make every aesthetic appraisal difficult, even impossible, because such a valuation presupposes in the first place real familiarity. Almost from the very beginning the Negro is seen as inferior and treated in an off-hand way, and whatever is put forward is taken, a priori, as inadequate. Judgement is based, carelessly, on a vague appeal to evolutionary hypotheses, which is then used to back up the spurious concept of the primitive, while others speak of this defenceless object with false phrases invoking the people from a time immemorial, and similar things. Thus one hopes to capture in the Negro a witness to origins, of a state that has never evolved. The majority of opinions on Africans is based on such prejudices in order to support a convenient theory. In his judgements on the Negroes the European retains one major postulate: his invincible, however exaggerated, superiority.

Such disrespect for the Negro is de facto born of our ignorance and the source of the unjust harm done to him.

Maybe from the plates of illustrations in this book one can deduce the following: that the Negro is not some being who has not evolved, that an important African culture has disappeared, and that the contemporary Negro corresponds to a possible 'antique' type as much as the Fellah of today does to an ancient Egyptian.

Some contemporary artistic problems have brought about a less trivial view of the art of the African peoples. As ever an actual artistic process has brought about its own history, and at its heart is the art of the African peoples. What had previously been seen as meaningless has taken on significance in the recent efforts of young sculptors, because it has been intuited that no one else has dealt with the precise problems of space and the formulation of the means of artistic production with such purity as the Africans. It also demonstrates that previous judgements on the Negro said more about the person so judging than about the object judged. In light of the new relation to this art there has also been the rise of a new passion: one now has collectors of African art for the sake of art, passionate in the sense that in such a justified activity one actually creates from the old material a new and significant object.

This brief presentation of African art cannot be, however, just extracted from the experience of contemporary art, no more than that which is taken as historically important is simply always a function of the immediate present. However, these relations will be dealt with later, to stay for the moment with one thing at a time, and not to confuse the reader with comparisons.

For the most part our knowledge of African art is slight and imprecise; apart from certain Benin works nothing is dated. Many works are described just on the basis of their find-place, which I think is really not of much use given the migration and intermingling in Africa and the fact that one can suppose that tribal conflicts, here as elsewhere, meant capturing the fetishes of the enemy and that the victor took the gods of the defeated to gain their force and protection. Completely different styles often come from the same region, for which various explanations might be offered, without preferring any one over the other. In this case one could say it was earlier or later art, two styles that co-existed, or another form of art which had been imported. In any case neither historical nor geographical factors allow one at present to have the slightest secure knowledge about this art. One might object and say that it is possible to establish chronological succession on the basis of an analysis of style by proceeding from the most simple to the complex. But one must take into account that it is illusory to think that the simple and the original must be identical; one is easily deluded in believing that there is a coincidence of beginning and method of thinking with the nature of the event. Every start (by which I mean an individual and relative beginning, as one cannot state any other kind) is extremely complex because man, even in one object, wants to express many things, even too much.

This must make it seem that to say something about African sculpture is a hopeless task. This is especially the case when the majority still require proof that this is art at all. One fears remaining completely in an external description which has no result other than stating a loincloth is a loincloth, and that no single thing can lead to a general conclusion as to what context these loincloths and pouting lips belong to (using art for anthropological or ethnographic ends seems to me dubious, since artistic representation says almost nothing about the facts to which these scientific disciplines are linked).

Despite all this one must proceed from the facts and not from some smuggled in surrogate. I believe there is something more certain than any kind of ethnographic knowledge and so on, and that is African sculpture! The object-ness of these works has been excluded in seeing them as emerging from an environment, and analysing them as figures which are so created. One attempts to establish from the formal characteristics of the sculpture whether there is a correspondence to the usual artistic forms. There is one thing that must be followed and another that must be avoided; one is that one must remain in vision and its specific laws, but not to substitute for vision or the creation that one is seeking the structure of its proper reflection; the other is that one must abstain from interpolating neat theories of evolution and make the process of thinking and artistic creation equivalent. One has to slough off the prejudice that supposes the psychic processes can be seen as the same situation under reverse signs, and that reflection on art is in opposition to artistic creation. This reflection is a generally different process which takes the question beyond form and its world, to integrate the work of art into a general becoming.

The description of the works as formal constructions has as a result something much more important than the description of the objects themselves; the objective itemization goes beyond the given creation in not treating it according to usage but as a guide to a praxis which is not at the same level. The analysis of form, on the other hand, remains in the field of the immediately given, since one has only a certain number of forms to account for, and these are taken as particular objects, help one have a better understanding, because more than just being forms they express the manner of seeing and the laws of vision, and thus grant a knowledge which remains in the sphere of the immediately given.

The possibility of such a formal analysis, which turns on the specific elements of the creation of space and of vision and which encompasses them, proves implicitly that these given creations are art. One could go so far as to state that the tendency to generalise and a given predisposition secretly already insists on such a conclusion. This is incorrect, because individual form contains the valid elements of viewing, represents them, so that they can be presented as form. The individual case does not disturb the character of the concept; there is, rather, a dualistic co-relationship. It is instead the case that it is the essential agreement between general viewing and the material realisation which brings about the work of art. Further we ought to consider that the creation of art is just as 'arbitrary' as the necessary tendency to bring to lawfulness individual viewing, where in both cases an organising process is pursued and achieved.

THE PAINTERLY

The habitual incomprehension of African art by the European is parallel to its stylistic power: an art which is a remarkable case of three-dimensional seeing (plastic vision).

It is possible to state that European sculpture is strongly imbricated with painterly surrogates. In Hildebrand's *Problem der Form* we possess an ideal balance between the painterly and the sculptural; such a remarkable art as French sculpture seems, up to the time of Rodin, to occupy itself with the dissolution of the plastic. Even frontality, which one habitually sees as the strict clarification, the primitive aspect of form, has to be considered as a pictorial anticipation of volume, because here the three-dimensional is concentrated on some planes which reduce the volume, and so one accentuates the parts closest to the viewer and orders them in consistent surface planes, while the more distant parts are taken as accessory modulations of the front surface which is dynamically weakened. One stresses the motif of objects placed in front. In other cases one replaces the three-dimensional with a concrete equivalent of movement or otherwise whittles away, by movement of the form, whether drawn or modelled, the essential: the immediate expression of the three-dimensional. The efforts of perspective are also harmful to the process of viewing.

So, one can easily understand that since the Renaissance the indispensable limits between free-standing sculpture and relief have been increasingly blurred, and that the exciting play of the painterly around mass, the cubic material, has invaded three-dimensional formal structure. As a logical consequence it has been painters and not sculptors who have pursued the decisive questions about the three-dimensional.

This makes clear why it is that our sculpture with its parallel formal developments has had to undergo a period of total blending of the pictorial and the plastic (Baroque) and that such a tendency must eventuate in the complete defeat of the sculptural, which has to resort, if it wants to retain the emotion of the creator and communicate it to the spectator, to entirely impressionistic and pictorial means. The three-dimensional was eliminated, and the individual script triumphed.

This history of form inevitably was linked to psychological processes. Artistic conventions were replete with paradox; harmony came from a totally emotionally driven creator and a completely abject viewer and it was the dynamics of the individual process which became the essential, and which was concentrated on and emphasised. The essential was what came before and would come after, and the work was increasingly reduced to a lightning conductor for psychological emotions, the individual flow, the cause and the effect were fixated. This sculpture was more an expression of the genetic development of objectified forms than the electric contact of two individuals, and the drama of the judgement about the artwork had a greater importance than the work itself. And it was necessary that every fertile canon of form and seeing had to be solved.

What results was an even more intense striving for the sculptural by a multiplication of means. The actual lack of the sculptural could not be made up for by the redolent fable of the 'touched up' model; instead what the legend showed was the absence of a complete and thorough conception of space.

Such actions destroy the distance towards things and value only the functional sense they preserve for the individual. This art is about the potential accumulation of the greatest possible functional effect.

Yes, indeed, we have seen in some recent artistic efforts that this potential component, the spectator, was made virtual and visible. Very few European styles diverged from this, notably the Romanesque-Byzantine, which nevertheless shows its oriental origin, and equally well-known is its quite rapid transformation into movement (Gothic).

The viewer was integrated into the sculpture, of which he became the indispensable function (for example in sculpture that was based on perspective). He was inextricably tied to the psychological re-evaluation of the creator's person, as long as he didn't contradict that person by judging him. Sculpture then was the stuff of conversation between two people. What inevitably is of interest to a sculptor with such an orientation is to determine in advance the effect and the viewer: in order to anticipate and try out the effect the sculptor has to turn himself into the viewer. (Futurist sculpture) and the sculpture has to be seen as a periphrasis of the effect. The spiritual, temporal component completely overwhelms the spatial determinants. To achieve this – often unconscious – aim the artist establishes identification of viewer and creator, for this was the only way to achieve the unlimited effect.

What is significant in this state of affairs is that the effect on the viewer is what is marked, even if it is of a weak intensity, as the reverse of the creative process. The sculptor submitted to the majority of spiritual processes and transformed himself into the spectator. Even during the course of working he would take continuous distance from his own work, which is that of the viewer, and model the effects. Displacing the centre of gravity to the viewer's visual activity, he modelled in touches so that it was the viewer who would shape the actual form. Spatial construction was sacrificed to the secondary, indeed alien feature of material motion and the precondition of all sculpture, three-dimensional space, was forgotten.

For some years now we have experienced the impact of the decisive crisis in France. By a real exertion of awareness the dubiousness of the process was recognised. Some painters had enough resolve to prevent their handwork from sliding any further into the merely mechanical: detaching themselves from the usual means and methods they investigated the elements of viewing space, to find out what viewing requires and demands. The result of these important efforts is sufficiently well known. At the same time, and quite logically, one discovered Negro sculpture, recognising that in its isolation it had cultivated pure sculptural forms.

The efforts of these painters is referred to commonly as abstraction and it cannot be denied that it was only by rigorous critique of the confused terminology that they could get closer to a direct grasp of space. But what is essential and separates Negro sculpture from such art, which takes African art as point of reference and acquires a similar awareness, is that what looks here like abstraction is an immediate and natural given in African art. Negro sculpture will prove to be in the formal sense the most powerful realism.

The contemporary artist does not seek only for pure form, he pursues it in opposition to his pre-history and ends up often interweaving through his efforts excessive reaction, whereby his necessary critique empowers the analytic character of his art.

RELIGION AND AFRICAN ART

African art is above all determined by religion. Sculpted work is venerated as it was by the people of antiquity. The maker fashions his work as if it were the divine or its guardian, which is to say that from the very beginning he is situated at a distance from the work, which is a god or its container. His work is adoration at a distance, and so the work is a priori something autonomous, more powerful than its maker, particularly since he directs his entire intensity to the work and thus as the weaker being he sacrifices himself to it. This work must be described as religious service. The work is a deity, free and independent of everything else; both worker and worshipper are at an immeasurable distance from the work. The latter will never be mixed up with human events except as something powerful and distanced. The transcendence of the work is tied to and presupposed by the religious. It is created in adoration, in terror before God, a terror which is also its effect. The maker and the worshipper are a priori spiritual, which is essentially identical; the effect lies not in the art work but in the posited and undisputed godliness. The artist does not dare compete with God in striving for an effect, this is a sure given and predetermined. There is no point in striving to treat the art work as trying for an effect, since the idols are often worshipped in darkness.

The artist realises a work which is independent, transcendent and not interwoven with anything else. To this transcendence corresponds a vision of space which excludes every function of the spectator. One has to have a space which guarantees that it is completely drained, a total space and one that is not fragmentary. The autonomous and closed space does not here signify abstraction but immediacy of sensation. This closure is not guaranteed unless the volume is fully rendered, and until one can add nothing further to it. The activity of the spectator does not come into question. (When it has to do with religious painting, the latter limits itself to the surface of the image to achieve the same end. One cannot get closer to this painting via the ornamental or decorative, as these are secondary consequences.)

I have said that the three dimensional needs to be rendered perfectly and without restriction, that vision is predetermined by religion and reinforced by a religious canon. This determination of the seeing brings about a style which is not subject to the will of the individual. On the contrary this style is canonically settled and only upheavals in the religious order could modify it. The faithful often adores the objects in darkness, in his devotions completely absorbed by his god, and is so given over to this that he hardly has any influence on the art work, to which he barely pays attention. It is the same thing when one represents a king or tribal chief, even in the effigy of the common man one sees and venerates a divine principle, which here again determines the work. In such art there is no place for the individual model or the portrait, since, like a profane accessory, it can hardly depart from the artistic practise of religious work or be contrasted with it, because it is a domain of little importance, hardly considered. The work is erected as a type of the adored power.

What characterises African sculpture is a strong autonomy of the parts, and this is also fixed by a religious rule. The orientation of the parts is not according to the function of the viewer but as a function of themselves. They are perceived in terms of compact masses and not at a weakening distance, thus, it is they themselves, and their limits, which one finds reinforced.

Another point of note is that the majority of these works have no pedestal or similar exhibition accessories to show them. This is likely to astonish us because to our mind these statues are highly decorative. Here, on the contrary, a god is never shown except as an autonomous being who has no need of any props. He does not lack pious and respectful hands as it is brought in by a procession of its worshippers.

Such an art rarely materialises the metaphysical, since it is taken for granted. The metaphysical has to be manifested in the perfection of the form and shown there in incredible intensity, which is to say that the form is developed to the point where it is fully self-enclosed. As a result there is powerful formal realism, for nothing else can release the forces so thoroughly, in their immediate form, and certainly not attempting this via abstract or reactive polemics. (The metaphysics of contemporary artists points to the earlier critique of the painterly, and busies itself with representation as a concrete and formal essence, which completely challenges the absoluteness of religion and art, and their strongly demarcated correlation is effaced in destructive confusion. In formal realism, by which one does not mean a naturalistic mimesis, the transcendental is given, imitation is excluded. How could one imitate a god, and to whom should a god submit? It follows from this there is a consistent realism of transcendent form. The art work is not seen as a product of arbitrary and artistic creation, rather more as a mystical reality, more powerful than natural reality. The art work is real on account of its closed form, and the fact that it is independent and above all powerful; the sense of distance is bound to produce an art of awesome intensity.

Where European art submits to interpretation according to feelings as well as according to form, in so far as the spectator has to have an active optical function, African art, for formal reasons, and religious ones too, has only one possible interpretation. It signifies nothing, it is not a symbol; it is the god which keeps his enclosed mythic reality, in which is also included the worshipper, transforming him into a mythic being too and abolishing his human existence.

The finite, closed form and religion correspond with one another, in the same way as formal realism and religious realism. The European work of art has become appropriately the metaphor of effect, which provokes the spectator to easy freedom. The religious art of Negro sculpture is categorical and is pregnant with essence which excludes all limitation.

To enter into the presence of such art one must exclude every temporal function, which means that one must prevent circling around the work, that one cannot touch it. The god is not in becoming, this would place his definite existence in question. It is necessary then to find a form that expresses itself immediately in solid material, and without the model, which betrays an impious hand. The vision of space which such a work of art manifests absorbs the space of three dimensions and expresses a unity, where perspective and the usual frontality is forbidden, that would be impiety. The work of art gives a general equation of space because by excluding all interpretation based on the temporal, founded on representations of movement, it becomes atemporal. It absorbs time in integrating in its proper form that which we experience as movement.

THREE-DIMENSIONAL SPATIAL VISION

It is a fact that any conceptual engagement, however anchored in the act of viewing, asserts its independence, and because of its specific structure, does not express all the divergences in artistic coming into being.

In the first place it is necessary to examine the formal nature of vision, which is the base of African art. We can now leave aside the metaphysical correlate, as we have shown that it is a constitutive element of the art work and we know that it is precisely from religion that it derives its absolute form.

We return thus to examine in formal terms the vision which shows itself in this art. We must avoid the error of mutilating African art in supposing that it is an unconscious memory of some European artistic form, since on the basis of form, African art appears to us as a specifically confined domain.

African art manifests a fixing of pure plastic vision. In the eyes of the naïve, the sculpture, which has the task of rendering in three dimensions, appears to be completely self-evident because it works on mass, which is itself defined by the three dimensional. This task seems at first difficult, and even insoluble, when one thinks that one has to render in terms of form, and not any specific spatiality, but three-dimensional space. When one reflects on it, one is seized by an almost indescribable emotion: these three dimensions, which one cannot grasp in a single look, have to be rendered not by some optical sleight of hand but shaped as complete and real expression. The solution of the Europeans when confronted with African sculpture is a series of opportunistic expedients, with which we are familiar, and which are only convincing in a mechanical and rote fashion. The usual devices are frontality, multiple points of view, the touching up of the model (overall relief), and the use of the sculptural silhouette.

Frontality almost robs the viewer of the volume by concentrating the expressive forces on one side. It arranges the parts in front in terms of a viewpoint and gives them a certain plasticity. The simplest, naturalistic perspective is chosen, the side that lies closest to the viewer, with which he normally orients in concrete life and in the psychological domain. The other aspects, the secondary ones, suggest in their rupture of the rhythm the sensation of movement in the three-dimensional. These abrupt movements, essentially tied together by the object, give rise to a homogeneous conception of space which is not justified at the formal level.

The same goes for the viewer in regard to the silhouette which, perhaps supported in all possible ways by perspective tricks, makes the volume present. On closer inspection we can see that the silhouette comes out of drawing, which is never a plastic element.

In all of these cases one finds either a painterly or graphic procedure. Depth is suggested but rarely given immediately as form. These processes are based on the following prejudice: that volume in three dimensions is guaranteed by the material mass, and that an inner emotion capable of circumscribing it, or a partial indication of form, is enough to make the volume exist as form. These methods try to indicate and suggest form rather than actually arriving at the logical consequences. However, from such a manner of proceeding it is hardly possible for the volume to be represented as mass and not directly as form. In any case mass is not equivalent to form, since mass, in effect, cannot be perceived as a unity; these processes always involve psychological acts which decompose the form into something evolving and thereby abolish it. This is the beginning of the difficulty: how to fix the visual act into an optical representation and to perceive it as a totality, fixing it in such a way that it can be seized in a single act of integration? But, what then is form in the volume?

It is clear that form has to be grasped in one go, not as a suggestion coming from the material. Rather, what is taken as movement must be fixed to the absolute. The elements situated in the three-dimensional have to be represented simultaneously, that is to say that the dispersed space must be integrated into a single visual field. The three-dimensional cannot be, and ought not to be, rendered simply by mass. It is necessary on the contrary that it be concentrated as a definite existent so that which engenders vision of the three-dimensional, and which is felt habitually and naturally as movement, is expressed by an immobile form.

Every point of intersection of three dimensions in the mass can be interpreted *ad infinitum*, which seems to present then insoluble difficulties for any univocal interpretation, and makes striving for totality seem impossible; even the relation of the point with the mass only serves to make the hope of a precise solution more difficult, because if one thinks to flatter the viewer with a precise homogeneous impression via a function one has introduced bit by bit and slowly, nevertheless no rhythmic ordering, nor the relation to drawing, nor the multiplication of movement, no matter how rich, can bring us to believe that the ensemble of the volume here is given and immediate and complete form.

The African has found, it seems, a pure and valuable solution for this problem. He has found, which appears paradoxical to us, a formal dimension.

The representation of volume as form, since it is only with this and not with the material mass that the sculptor has to work, was the immediate result of the need to determine what constitutes form; the parts that are not simultaneously visible had to be united with the part which places the viewer in a single visual act and which corresponds to an established three-dimensional vision – even given that the volume which is nonetheless irrational insists on itself as something visible and formed. The optical naturalism of Western art is not an imitation of external nature; nature here is passively imitated and given to the viewpoint of the spectator. Thus one understands the genetic process and its terribly relativistic consequences, which is a feature of most of our art. This is a conformity to the viewer (frontality, image at a distance) and more and more the creation of a definitive visual form is given over to the active and co-operative viewer.

As with our representation, form is an equation. This equation has an aesthetic value if it is understood in an absolute fashion, and without any relation to external elements. Form is the perfect identity of vision and a specific realisation, which in virtue of their structure coincide perfectly, and do not have the same kind of connection as that between a concept and a particular fact. Viewing may encompass many cases of realisation, but does not, nevertheless, have a level of reality greater than these instances. It is thus clear that art represents a particular case of unconditioned intensity and it must engender quality in its complete integrity.

It is the mission of sculpture to form an equivalent which totally absorbs the entirely naturalistic sensation of movement, to take mass and transform its diversity and succession into a formal order. This equivalence has to be total so that the art work stops being misprised as the result of human tendencies directed elsewhere, but instead, as something independent, absolute and enclosed.

The normal dimensions of space are three in number, but the third, the dimension of movement has only been enumerated and not analysed in its essence. If we accept that the work of art extracts from simple nature, then we see that the third dimension is bifurcated. We think of motion as a continuum which in its modulations encloses space. Given also that sculptural art fixates, this unity is sundered; that is to say it is taken in two different directions and encloses the two completely different directions, which remain unimportant in terms of the infinite space of the mathematician. Depth and the forward tendency in sculpture are thus two totally different ways to produce space. The distinction is not on the linear plane; there is rather a difference in fundamental forms – when not inextricably entwined in the impressionist fashion – that is to say, once more under the influence of naturalistic representations of motion. From this it follows that sculpture is in a certain sense discontinuous even if one cannot identify the fundamental means via the contrasts by which space is created in its totality. The volume does not have to be viewed as a secondary suggestive relief and should not be introduced as only a materialised relationship, but ought in fact to be posited as an essential being.

Whoever looks at sculpture is led to believe that his impression is made up of vision and also a representation which he makes of parts that are placed in depth. Such an effect, given its ambiguity, has nothing to do with art.

We have already argued that sculpture has nothing to do with naturalistic mass, but only with clarification of form. It has to do with figuring the visible parts and the invisible ones in their formal function in the volume. The quotient of depth, as I like to call it, has to be shown as form; it is true as form alone, without mixing it up as the concrete mass. The parts do not have to be rendered in a pictorial fashion, but rather in such a way that the form which renders the sculpture, and which is given in natural movement, is fixed as a unity, visible simultaneously. In other words, every part has to find its plastic independence and be deformed in a manner that absorbs the depth as well as the representation, as if the verso appeared and integrates with the front side which nevertheless has a three-dimensional function. Thus every part is the result of a formal representation which creates space as a totality and as a perfect identity between the individual optic, the vision which rejects ad hoc surrogates that weaken space and thus reduce it to mass. Such a sculpture is strongly centred on a side, given that it renders the volume in its totality without deforming the cubic in its ensemble, while it accumulates everything only on the front plane. The integration of the plastic element is bound to produce functional centres, according to which it is ordered, and it is around these 'points centrales' [sic.] of volume that, necessarily, strong partitions occur which one could qualify as the power access points to the independence of the parts. This is understandable because natural mass plays no role, the famous integral mass of previous masterpieces is unimportant; on the other hand the figure is captured here not as effect, but on the contrary immediately, in its spatial existence. The body of god is extracted, the dominant one, and he escapes the confining hands of the workmen; the body is conceived in terms of its proper function. One often criticises African sculpture for its so called errors of proportion, until one understands that the optical discontinuity of space is translated into the clarification of the form in an ordering of the parts of which, because they have to do with plasticity, the diversity is evaluated according to sculptural expression. In the first instance it is not thus their size which is determining, but more the expression of volume which they strive to figure no matter what. What African sculpture always rejects, but which the European always favours because of the compromise he accepts is to make, by interpolation, relief the fundamental element of the purely plastic process, which necessarily needs a rigorous distribution of volume. The faces are in some ways subaltern functions, because the form has to be brought out concentrated and intensified in the volume in order to be truly form. And because the form is precisely represented independently of the mass as a result and expression, only that is permissible, because the relevant art in terms of quality is a question of intensity; the volume then has to show itself in the subordination of image as an intensity that is tectonic. This is the moment to approach the concept of monumentality, which is clearly the concept of periods which lack any vision, and assess their works in terms of the same measure. Since art is an affair of intensity, monumentality and scale disappear. There is another thing that has to be eliminated. It can never be allowed to approach these plastic arrangements by means of linear interpolations – this démarche reveals a visual faculty weakened by conceptual memories – nothing more. One understands the rigorous realism of the African if one learns to see how in regarding the restricted space the work of art is immediately fixated. The function of depth is precisely not expressed by measurement but as a result through the directional intertwining, and not the objectively additive spatial contrasts. The result can never be grasped globally in the representation of movement that gives mass, because the volume does not consist of separate parts situated in a different way; it is in their three-dimensionality they are grasped as an ensemble that has nothing to do with mass or the geometric line. It describes the existence of volume as an absolute result, without a becoming, since movement has been absorbed.

After this assessment of the plastic concentration, the consequences are easy to explain. It has often been objected that Negro sculpture lacks a sense of proportion, and by others asserted in reverse that one can read from it the anatomical structure of different tribes. Both these views can be set aside, because the organic element has no particular sense in art – as it only shows the effective possibility of movement.

In treating artistic critique and reflection about art as equal – reversing completely the order – one is forced to construct theories with concepts that lack any subtlety, as if art came from a model and could be straightforwardly deduced. It is obvious that the premise of such a process would already be art; in the course of the analysis one must never leave the level of the object, otherwise one ends up talking about everything but the object in question. Abstract or organic (be they conceptual or naturalistic) are criteria which are alien to art and therefore facts completely external to it. One must also abandon vitalist or mechanistic explanation with regard to artistic forms. Big feet are not large because they have the function of carrying, but rather our eyes are drawn down in that the artist seeks a balance that contrasts with the pelvis. Given that the form is not tied up with the organic element or mass, the majority of Negro sculptures have no pedestal (the organic necessity here and there requires a pedestal to form a contrast between geometry and density); when a pedestal exists, it is emphasised by points and so on.

Returning to the question of proportions, they depend on the force with which depth must be expressed on the basis of the depth quotient, by which I mean the resulting sculpture. The relation of parts between themselves depends exclusively on the value of their function in the volume. The important parts require an appropriate three-dimensional result. Thus one must understand the twisted articulation and the proportions of the limbs of the Negro sculptures; this contortion manifests in a visual and concentrated fashion the connecting of the volume produced by two contrasting directions, brusquely intermingled distant parts set back which one hardly notices and this becomes active and functional in the midst of an intense and concentrated expression – they become form and absolutely necessary to the immediate representation of volume. To these integrated parts it is necessary to subordinate the other sides according to an unusual coherence, so that they do not remain suggestive, but unworked material; they have taken an active part in the form. On the other hand the depth becomes visible as a totality. This form, which is identical to the unified viewing, expresses itself in constants and contrasts. But they are no longer open to an infinite interpretative possibility. On the contrary, the two-fold depth direction that is the forward and backwards movement is interwoven in the same three-dimensional expression. Every part of the three-dimensional volume can be determined in two directions. Where it is integrated and fixed, the resulting three-dimensionality is self-contained and not externally interpolated, and the relation of the two constants makes up the depth. One can see in Negro sculpture, as in other so called primitive arts, something which has been remarked upon: that some statues are unusually long and etiolated and the resulting three-dimensionality is not yet accentuated. Perhaps this is an effort to encompass via the stretched out form the volume in three dimensions. By reason of the surrounding space one has the impression of not being able to hold onto these concise and simple forms.

On the subject of group sculpture I will add only a few words. They confirm the opinion already stated that the volume is not expressed by its mass but by the form. Otherwise these statues would look like all porous statues, a paradox and a monstrosity. These sculptures represent the extreme case which I like to call 'the remote sculptural effect'; two parts of the group do not relate, when looked at more closely, other than as two stretched out parts of the same statue. Their unity is expressed as a subordination to a plastic integration, in supposing that there is not just a formal repetition of theme with whatever effect or contrast, or some additional effect. Contrasting repetition would have the effect of reversing the directional values, and also the meaning of sculptural orientation. The juxtaposition in fact shows in a simple visual field the variation of a sculptural system. The two processes are perceived as a totality because the given system is unique.

MASKS AND RELATED PRACTICES

A people for whom art, religion and morality are immediate powers, and who are dominated and encircled by such powers will make them visible in themselves. To scarify is to make one's body the means and end of vision. The African scarifies his body and gives it a new intensity; his body in a visible way is given over to the great All and this abandonment clothes him in sensible form. It is characteristic of a despotic religion and cult of humanity which is equally forceful to have men and women transformed by the marking of their individual body into a collective body, and thereby intensify their erotic force. What, one may speculate, goes on in the mind which can conceive its own body as an unachieved work to be transformed directly? The naturalistic body is what the tattoo reinforces and the tattoo attains its perfection when it denies natural form and replaces it with a superior imaginary form. In this case the body at best becomes both canvas and clay; it becomes an obstacle which provokes the maximum creation of form. The tattoo presupposes an awareness of the immediate self and a not less strong consciousness of the objective practice of form. Here one finds what I call sense at a distance, and a prodigious gift for objective creating.

Tattooing is only a part of the objectification of oneself which consists in exercising an influence on the entire ensemble of the body, to be produced consciously in public and not only in dance for example, an immediate expression of movement, or a fixed expression such as a hair-do. The Negro defines his type with so much force that he transforms it. Everywhere he intervenes to indicate a fixated expression which one could not feign. Anyone can understand the man who feels himself to be a cat, a river, the weather, transforms himself, and the consequences thereof which he implements in his all too unambiguous body.

It is thanks to the mask that the European versed in psychology and the art of the theatre comprehends the feeling best. A human being is always changing slightly and transforms himself a little. He tries however to keep a certain continuity, to preserve his identity. The European has made of this feeling a somewhat hypertrophied cult. The African, who is less a prisoner of the subjective me, who honours objective powers, has to change in tandem with these powers as he affirms them and especially when he celebrates them with the greatest fervour. By these transformations he establishes a balance with the adoration of these powers that risks obliterating him; he takes on the god, he dances for the tribe in ecstasy and transforms himself by means of the mask into the tribe and the god. The metamorphosis permits him to grasp radically that which is essential to him; he incorporates it and in the objectification that reduces to nothing he is every individual event.

That is why the mask has no sense if it is not inhuman, impersonal, that is to say when it is a pure construction of every individual experience. It is possible the Negro reveres the mask even when he is not wearing it.

I would like to put it like this: the mask is immobile ecstasy, perhaps also the fantastic stimulant always to hand, to evoke ecstasy, because it carries fixed in it the face of the adored power or animal.

One might be somewhat surprised to discover that arts which are so dominated by religion are so often beholden to the human figure. This seems to me easy to conceive because mythic existence independent of appearance is already a convention. The god is already inverted and his existence is indestructible, whatever appearance he takes. This almost contradicts the radical level of the artistic feeling, threatening to make it disappear at the level of concrete content rather than consecrate all its force on the adoration of form – the actual existence of the god. For only the form in art is the measure of the existence of the god. Maybe the worshipper wants to chain the god to the human in representing him as such, and perhaps in his piety bind him, for no one is so egotistical as the worshipper who certainly gives all to the god, but without even knowing that this creates man.

It is also the moment to explain the sculptural expression of masks. This fixity is nothing more than the highest degree of intensity of expression, liberated from all psychological origins, and at the same time it permits above all the elaboration of a clarified structure.

I have illustrated a series of masks, which goes from architectural masks to the simply human, to show the diversity of the aptitudes of the soul of the people.

It is almost at times impossible to determine the types of expression in the work of the African sculpture. Does it express the sublime, or provoke it? Here we have demonstrated the beautiful example of an ambiguity of the expression of feelings, and our own experience teaches us that two opposing sensations often result in an identical expression.

The animal masks impress me deeply as I think of how the African takes on the animal, which in other circumstances he kills. The god also dwells in the animal that has been killed and perhaps the African has the feeling of sacrificing himself when he is putting on the mask of the animal, he pays his tribute to the slain animal and gives thanks to approach closer to the god, in which he sees a power that is greater than himself: his tribe. Perhaps in so transforming into the slain animal he escapes a vengeance which would otherwise pursue him.

Between the human mask and the animal mask there is the mask which holds the power of auto-transformation. We touch here on mixed forms which despite their fantastic or grotesque content show a typical African balance. It is the religious fervour for which the visible world no longer suffices, which produces an intermediate world, and in the grotesque affirms, menacingly, the disparity between gods and creatures.

I will not delay on stylistic interpretations of the African mask. We have seen how the African considers the sculptural forces and the visible results. In the masks is also expressed the force of a three-dimensional vision which affronts the surfaces, condensing all the back parts of the face into a few plastic forms and elaborating the elements least capable of expressing space into three dimensions.

PLATES

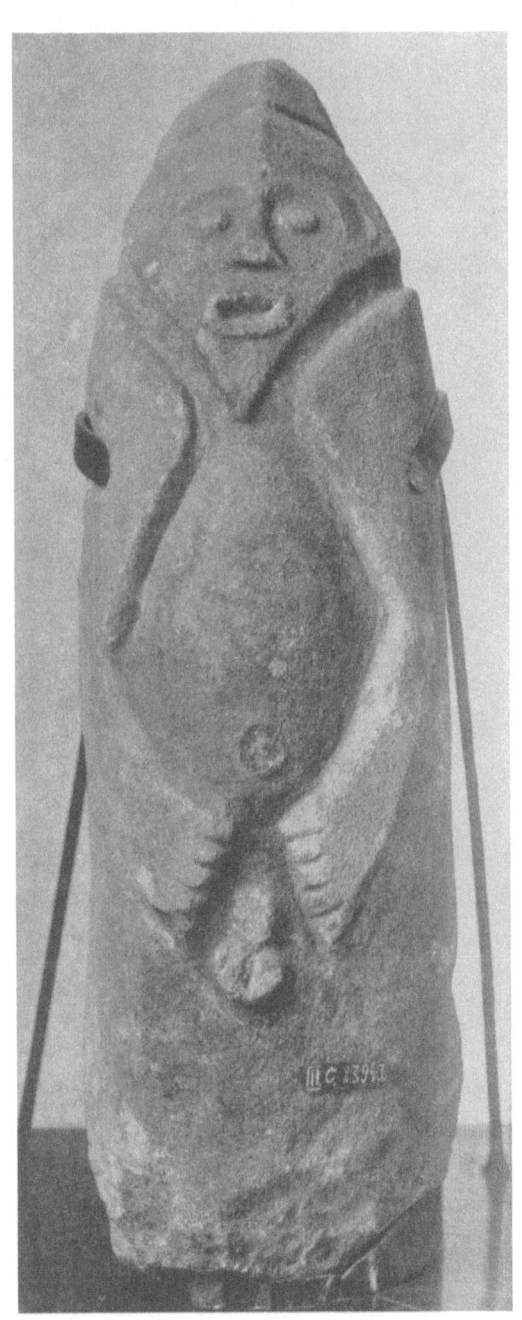

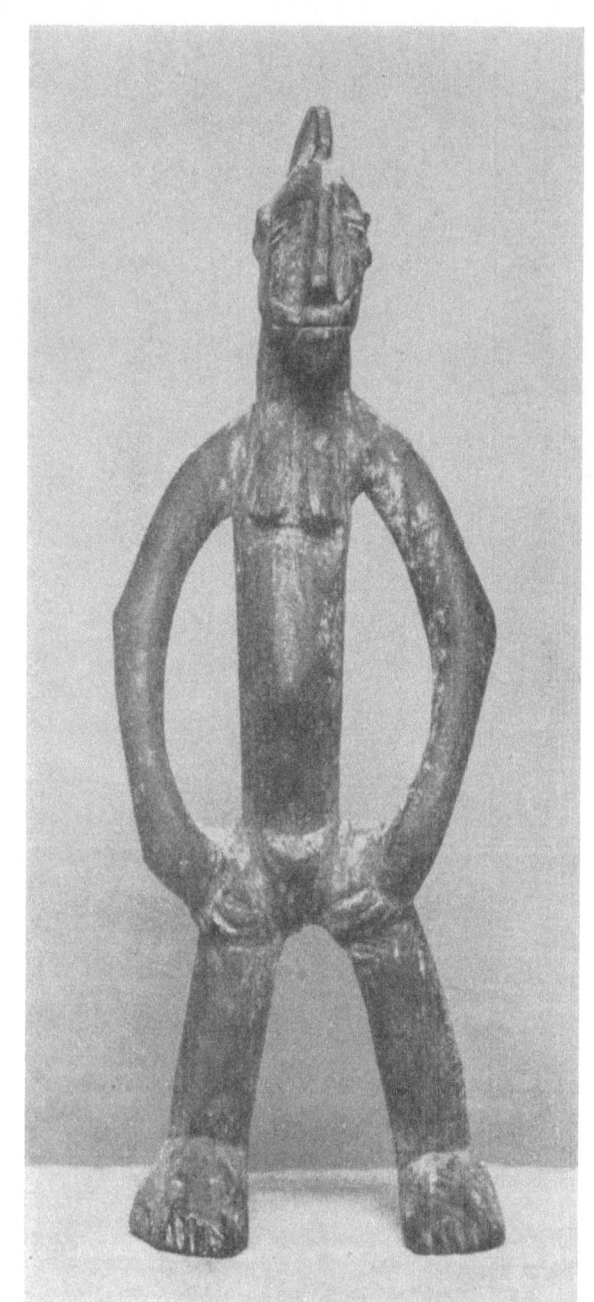

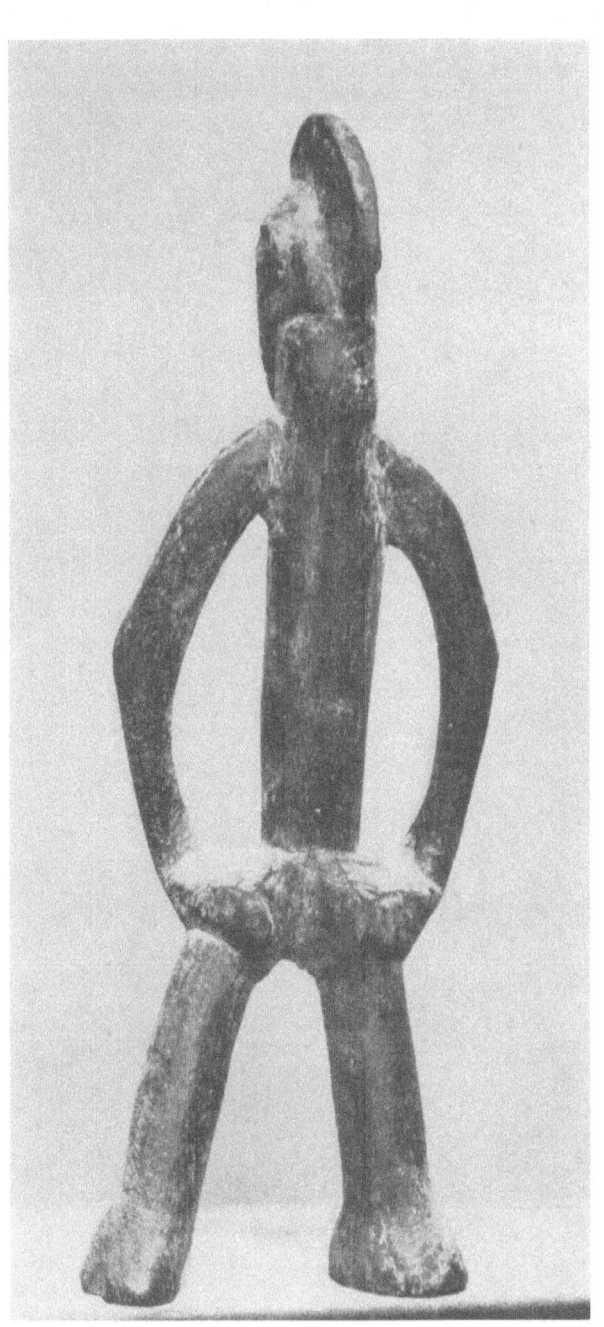

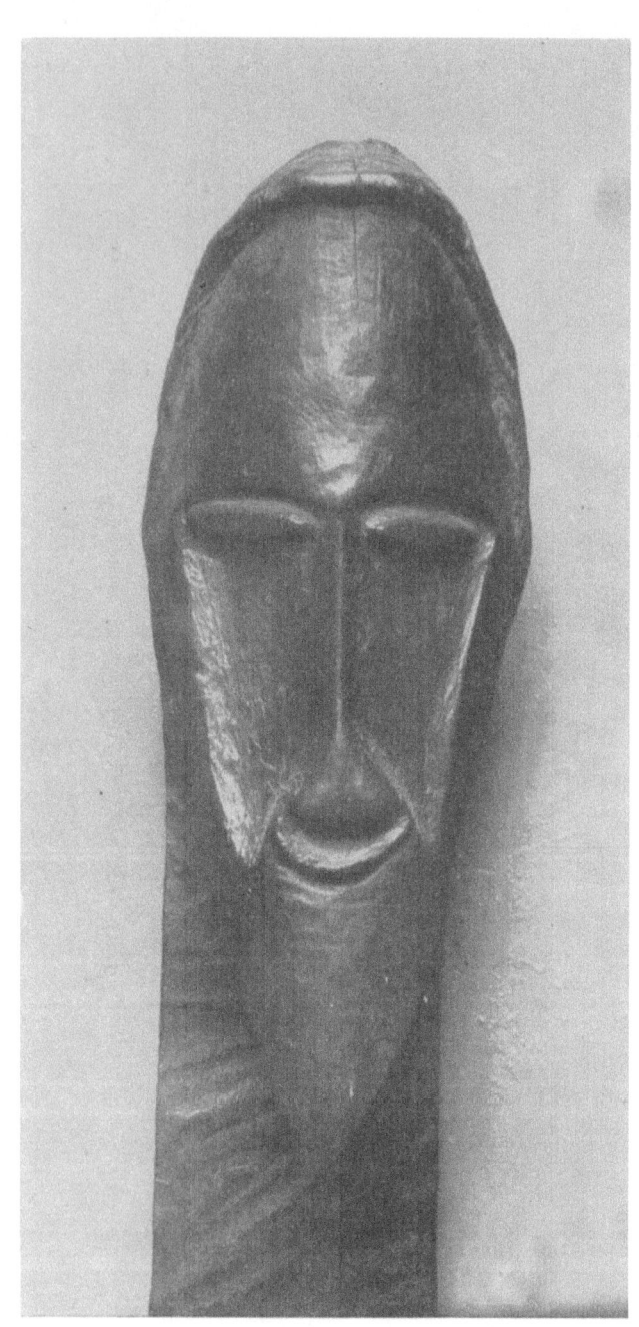

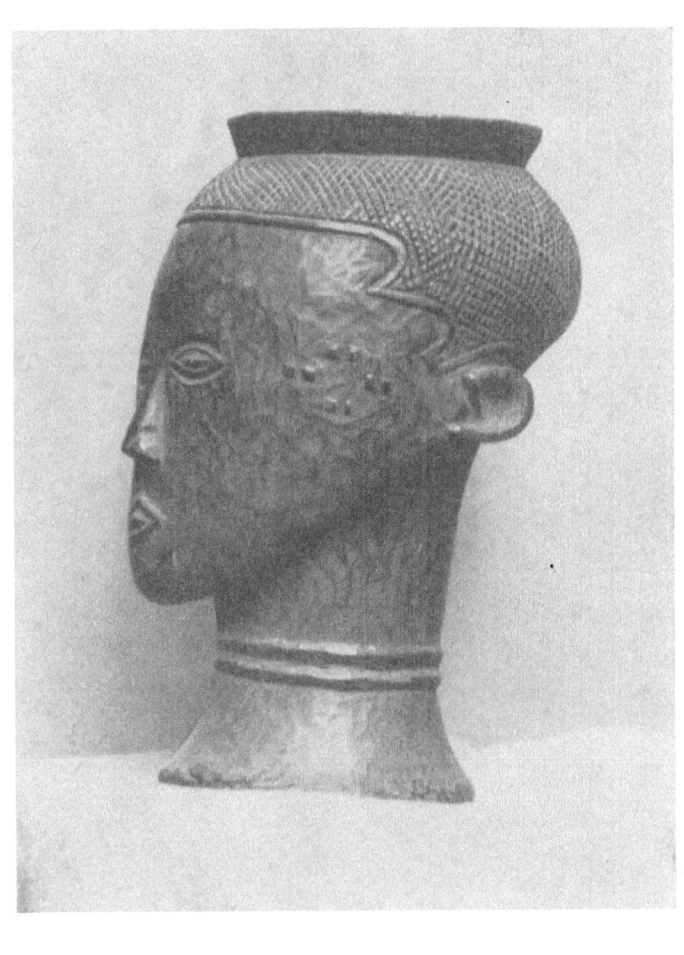

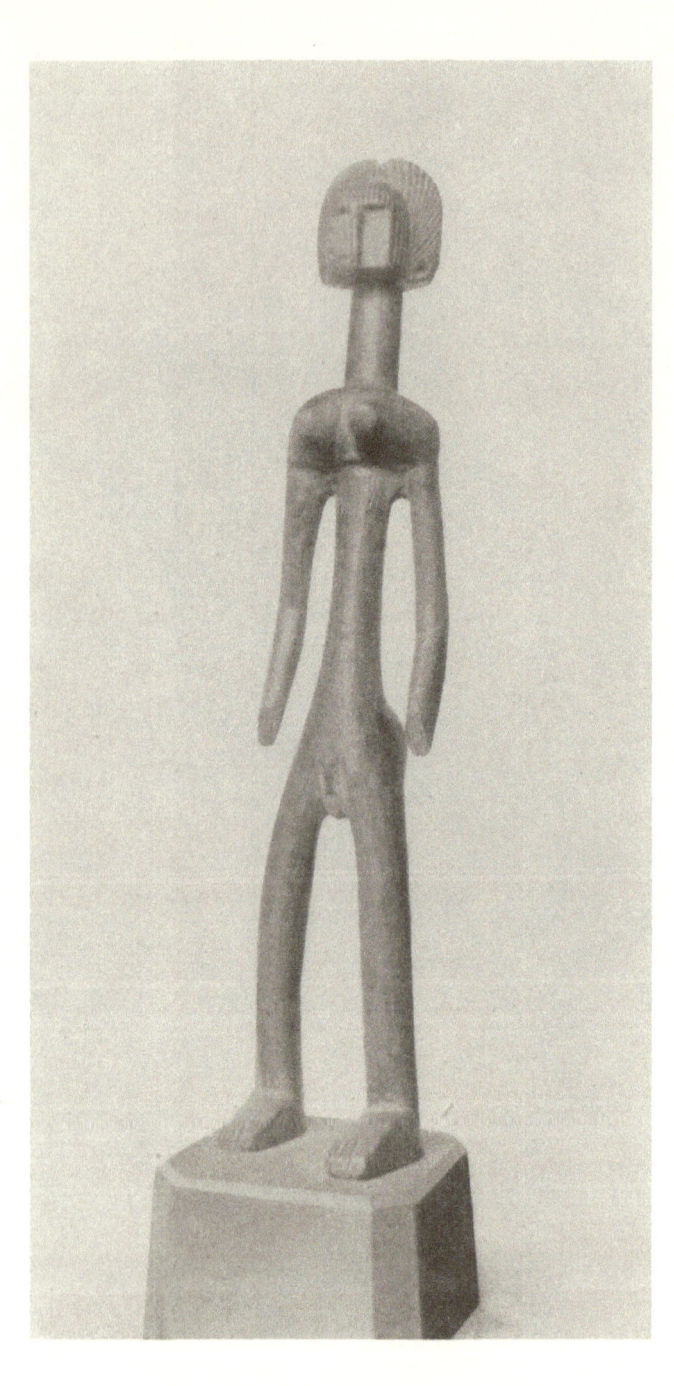

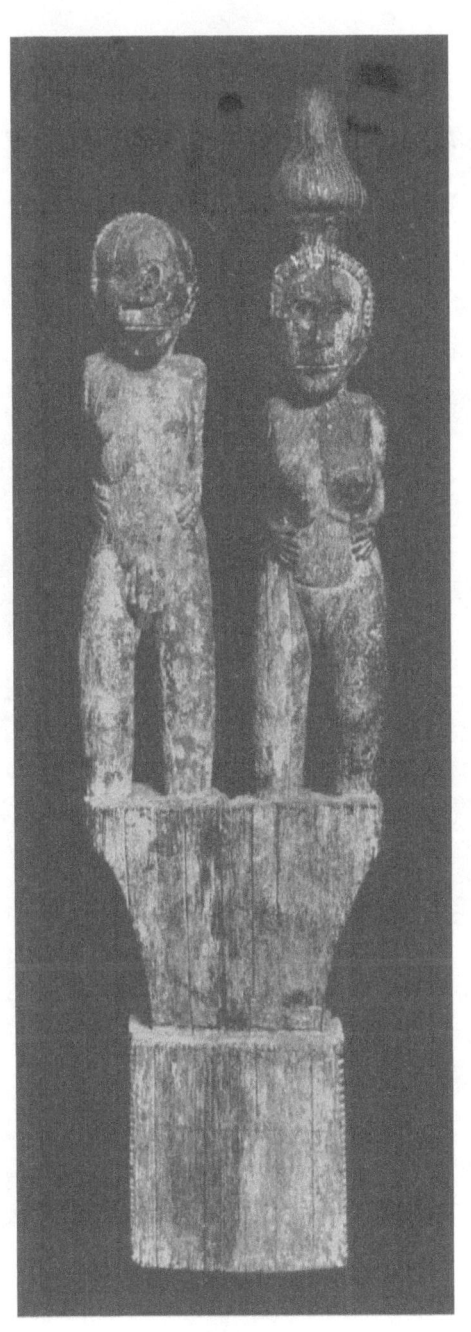

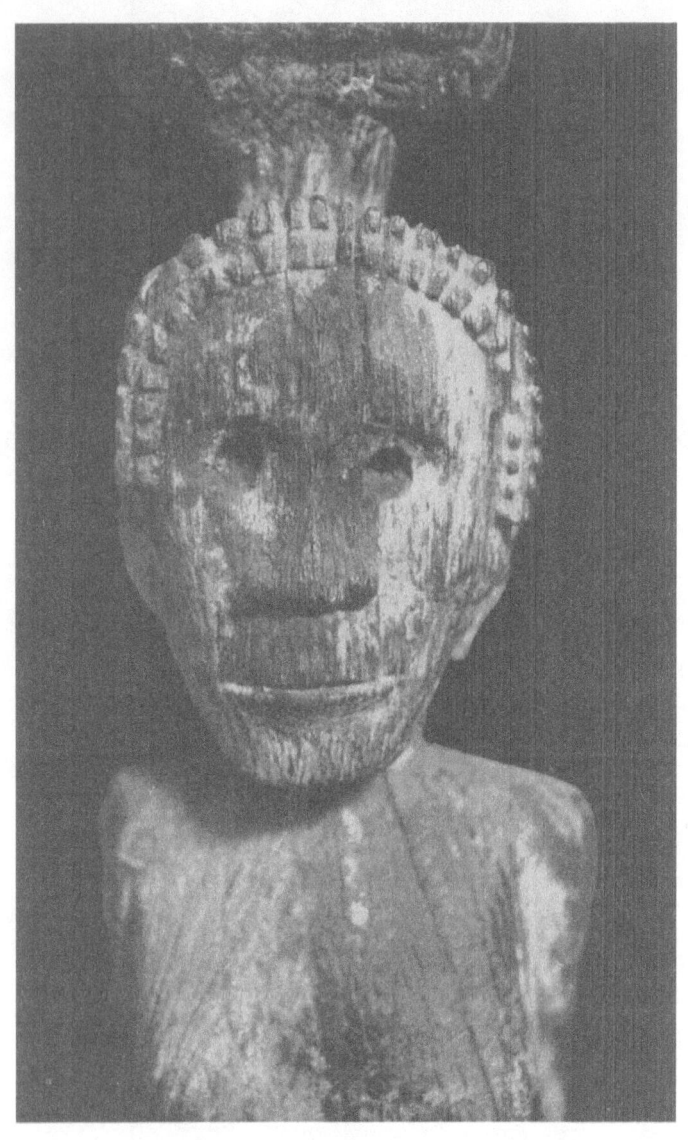

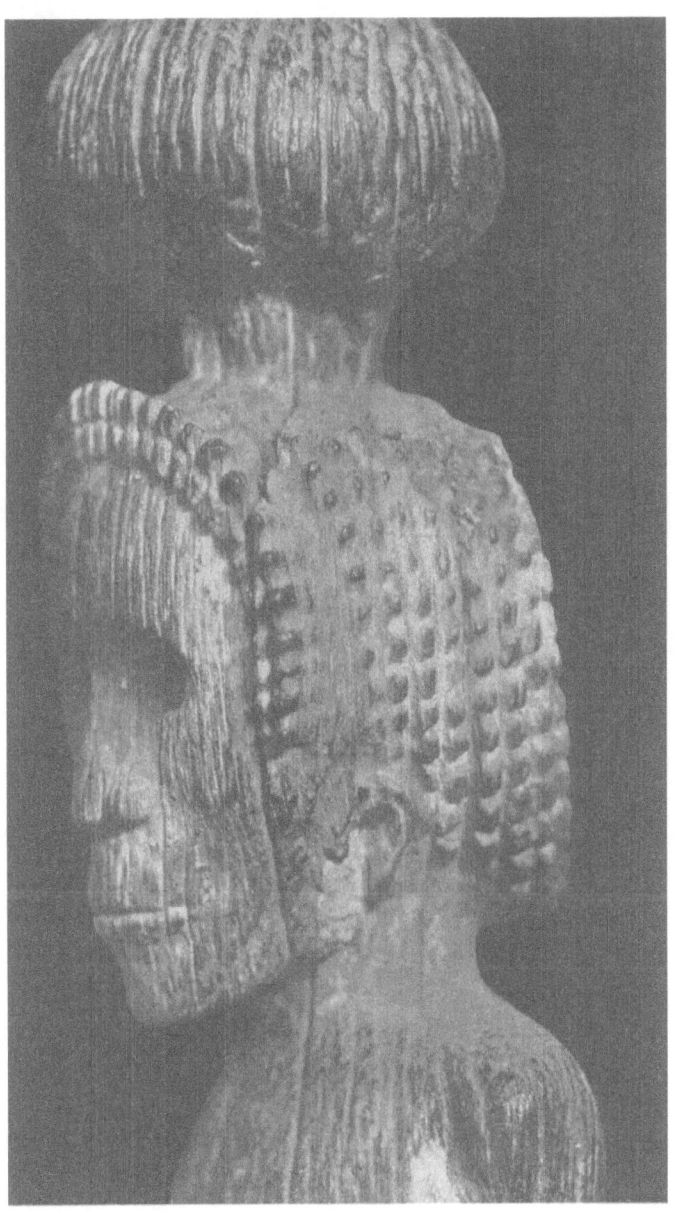

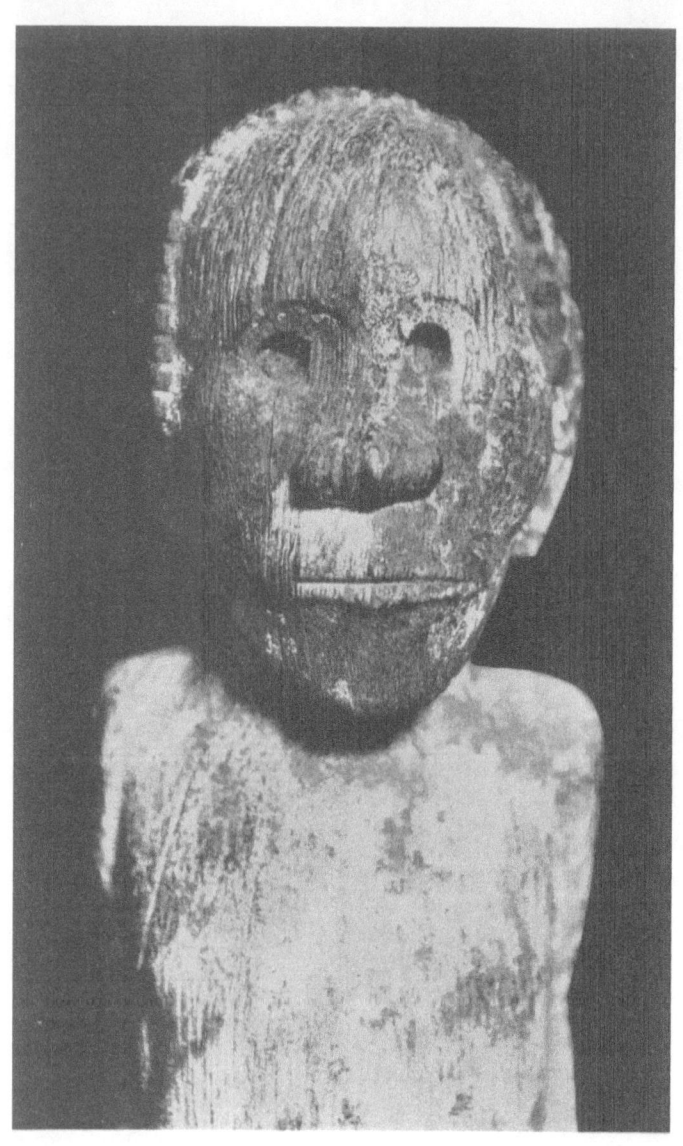

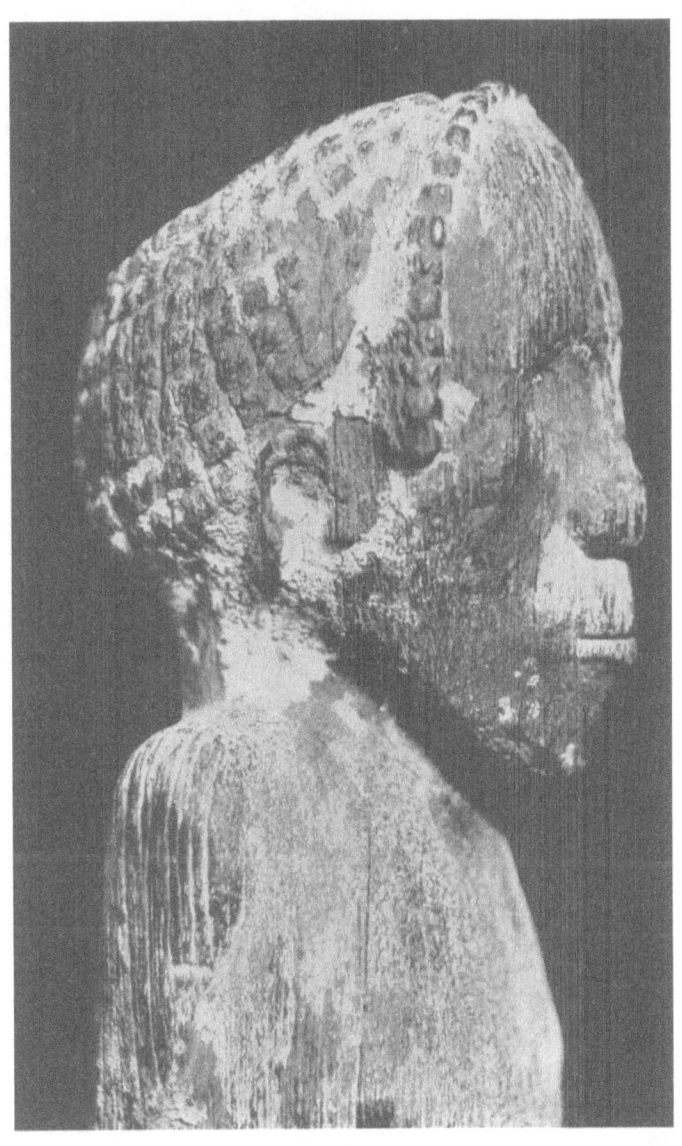

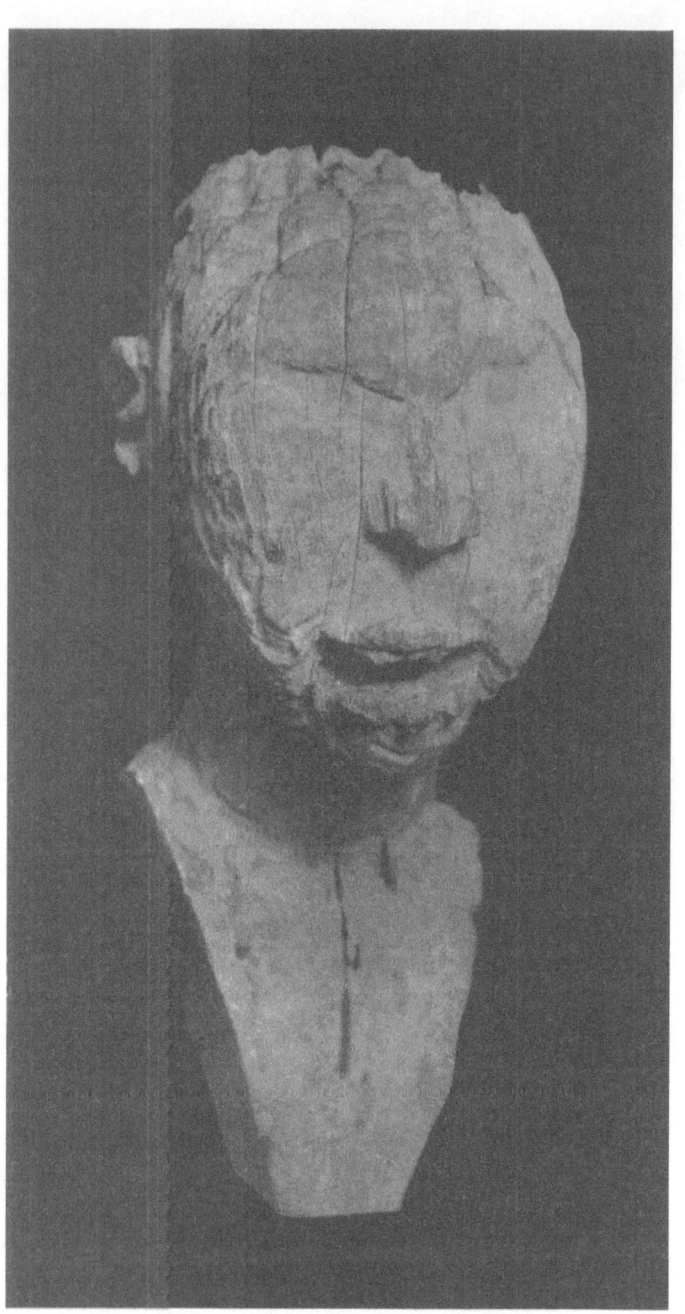

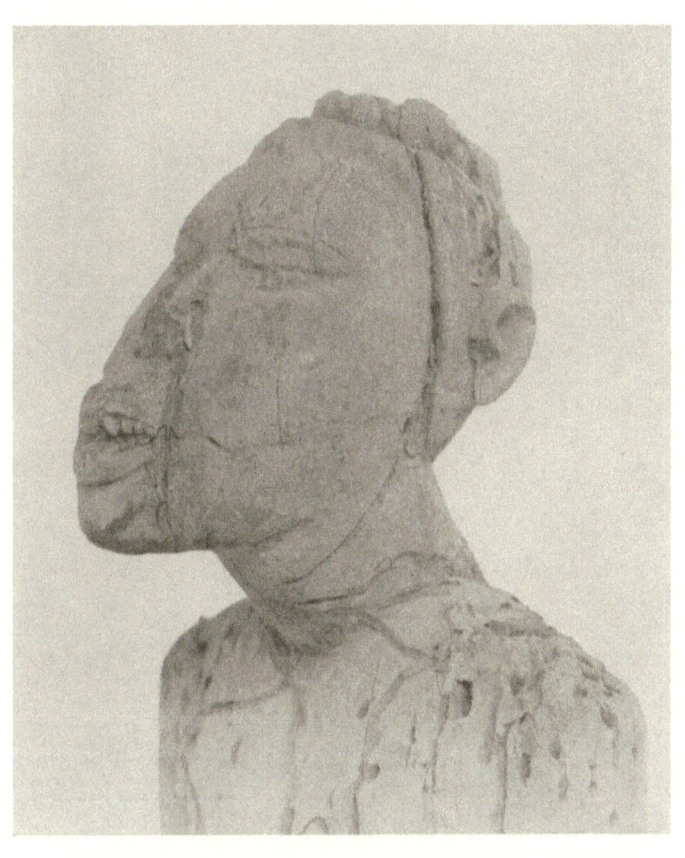

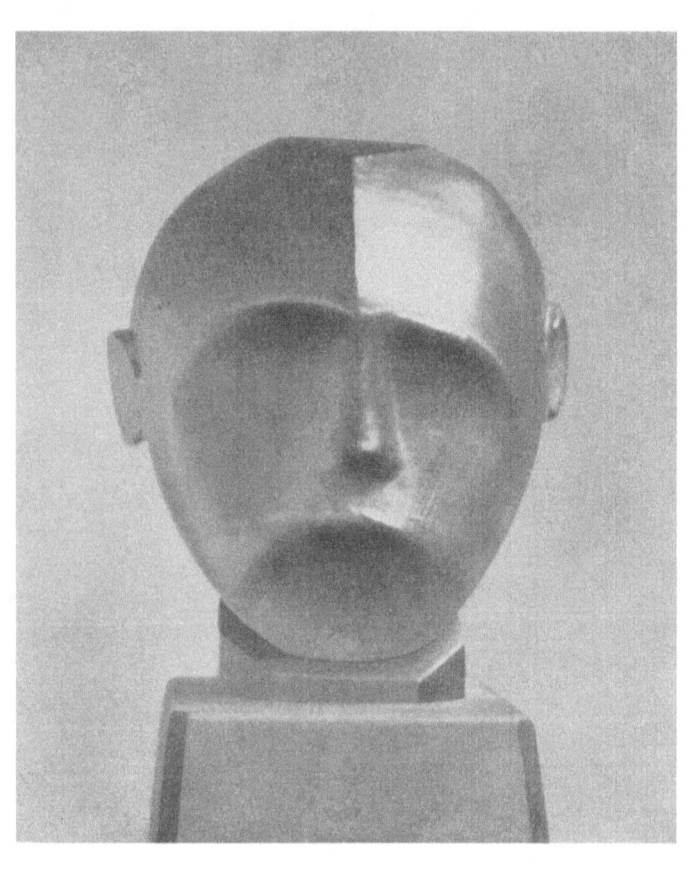

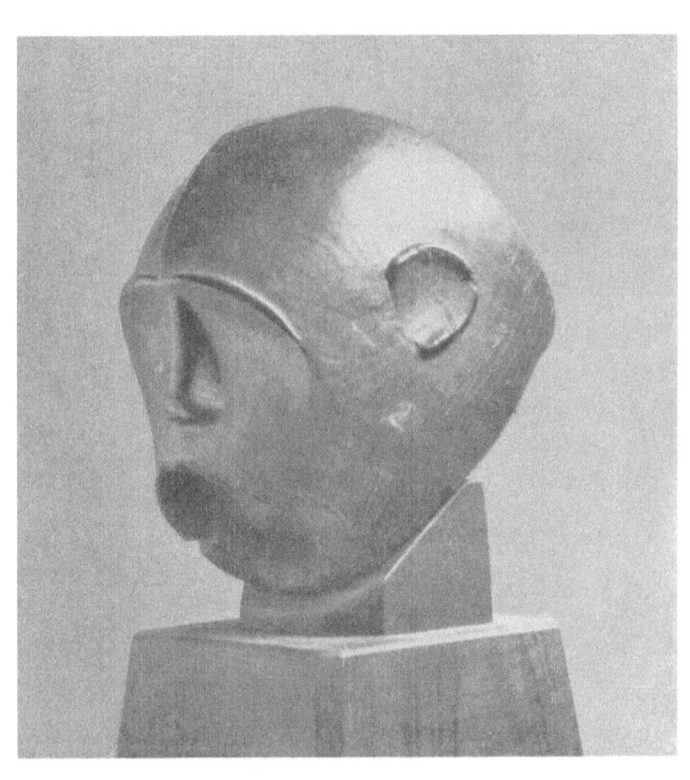

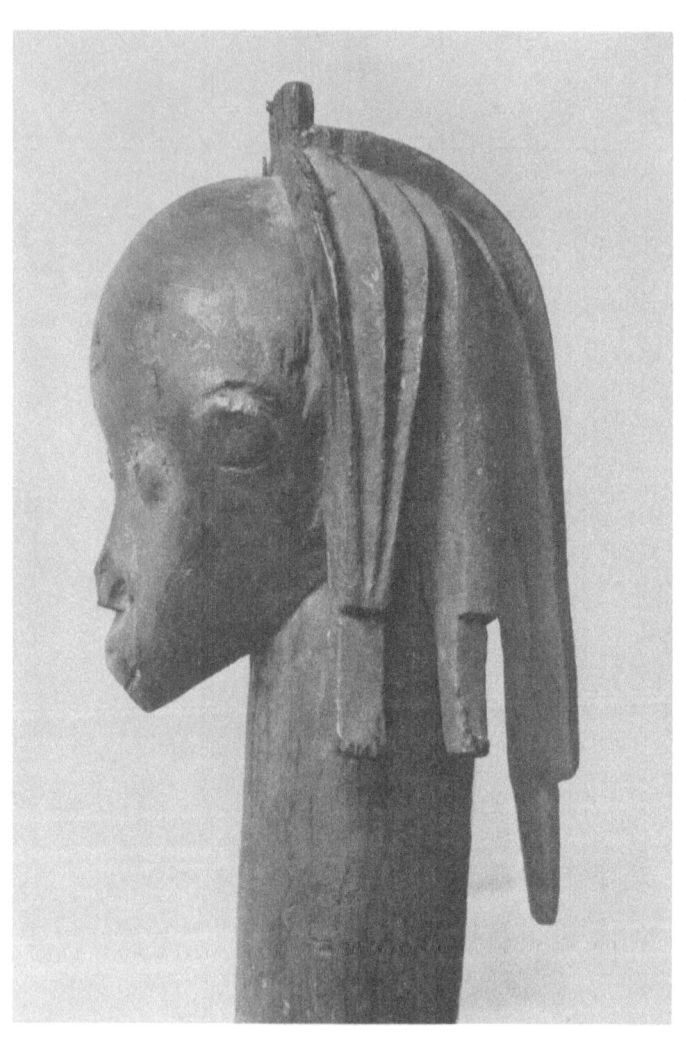

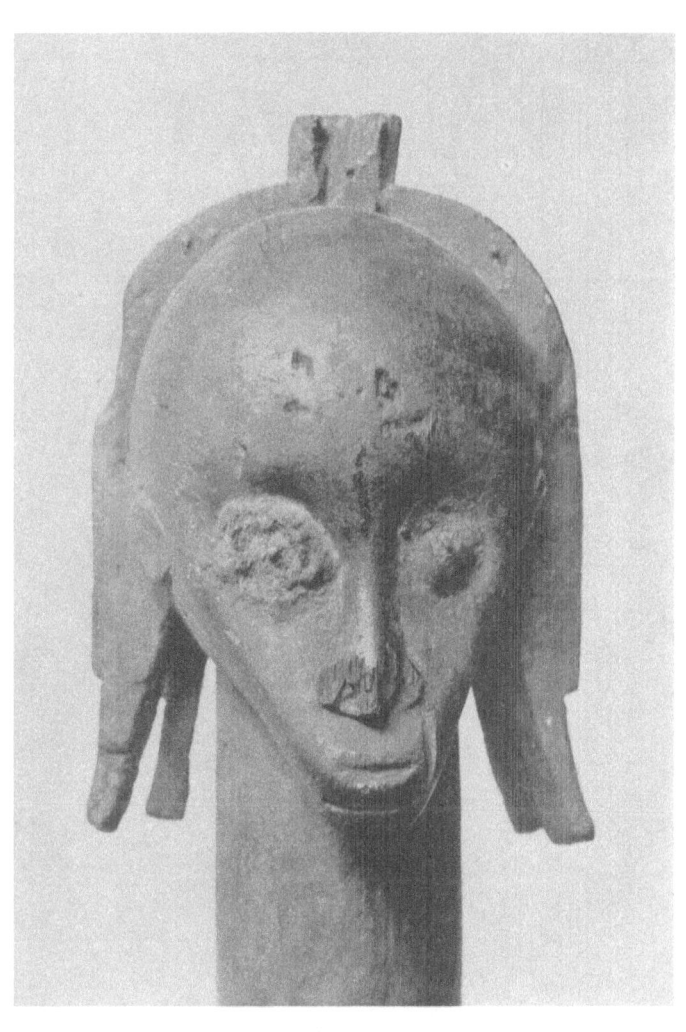

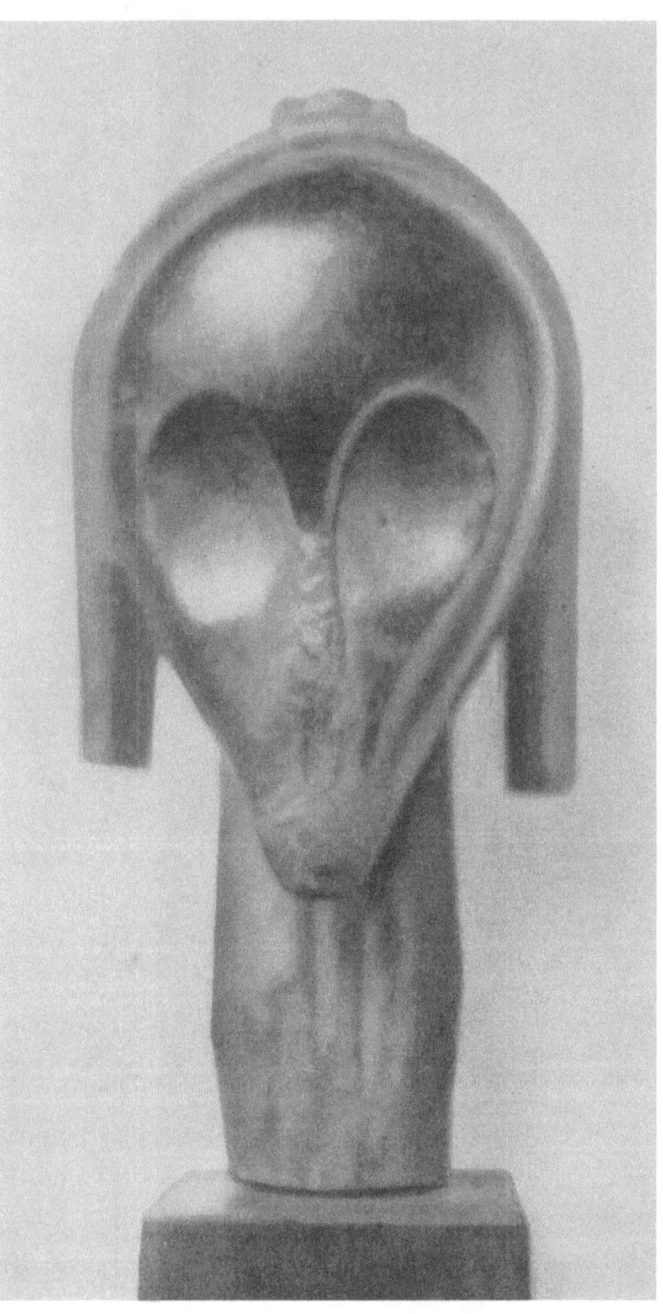

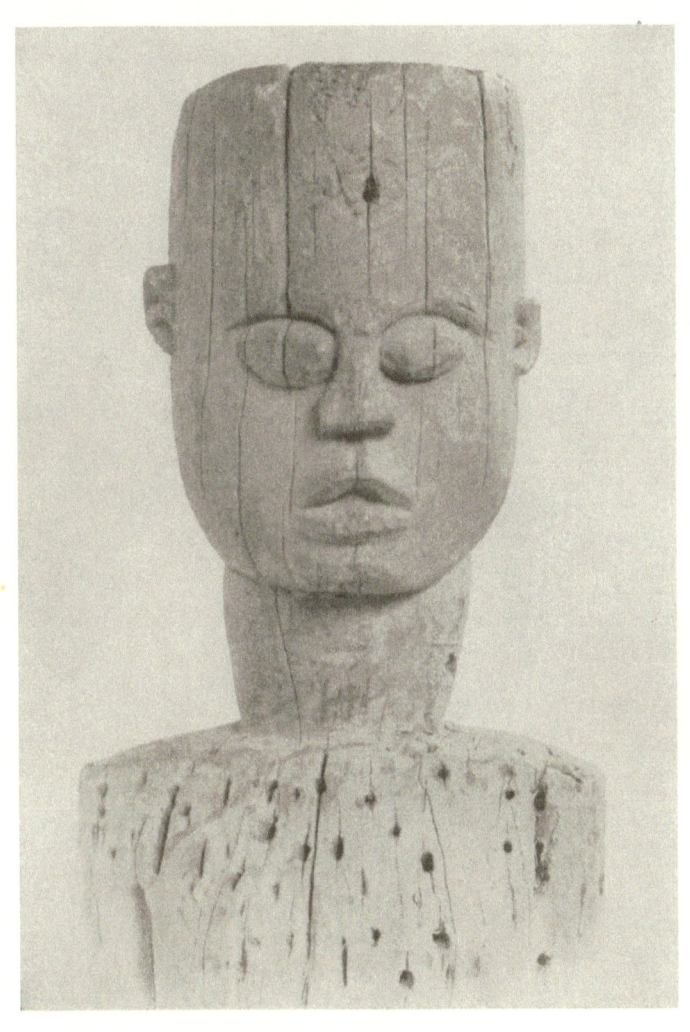

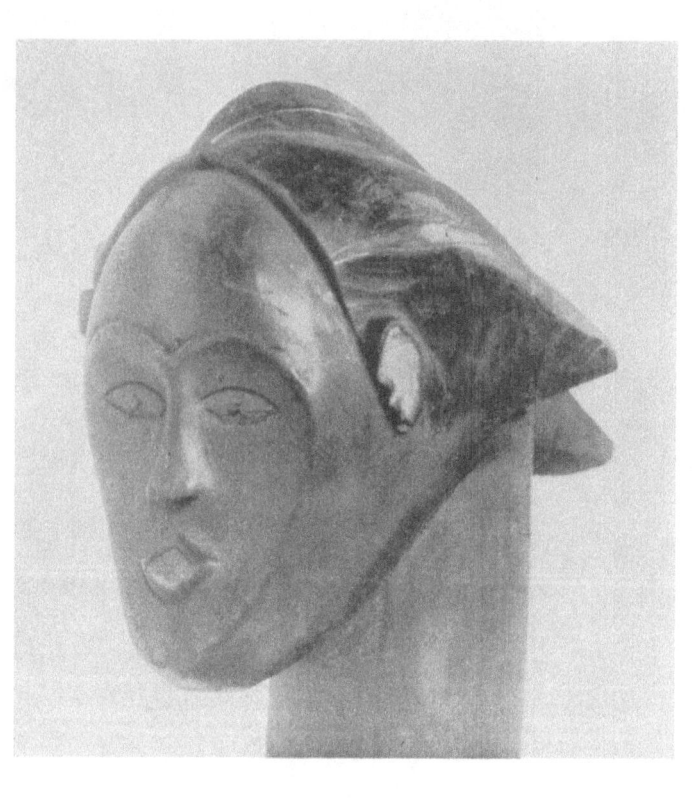

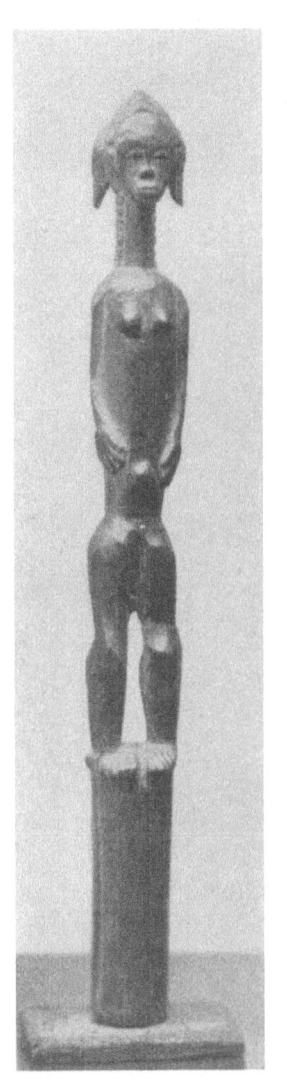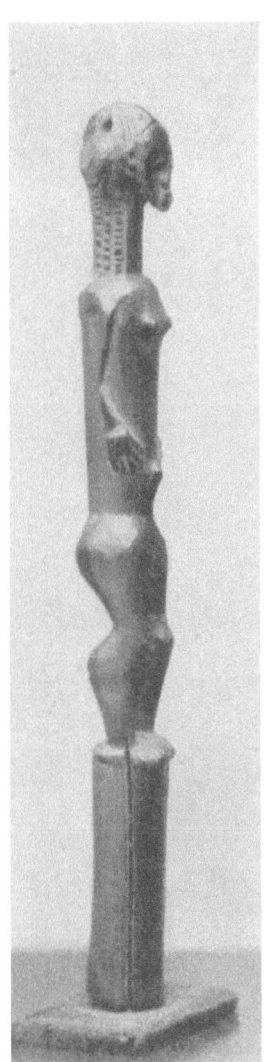

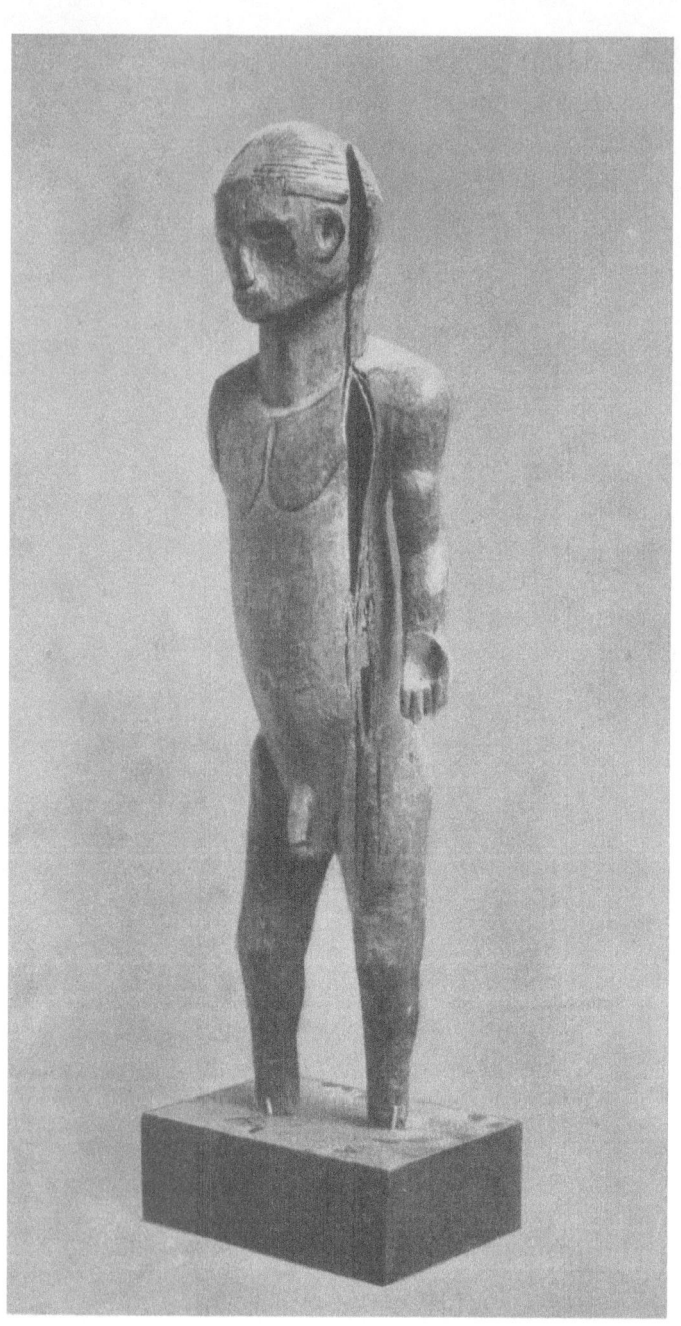

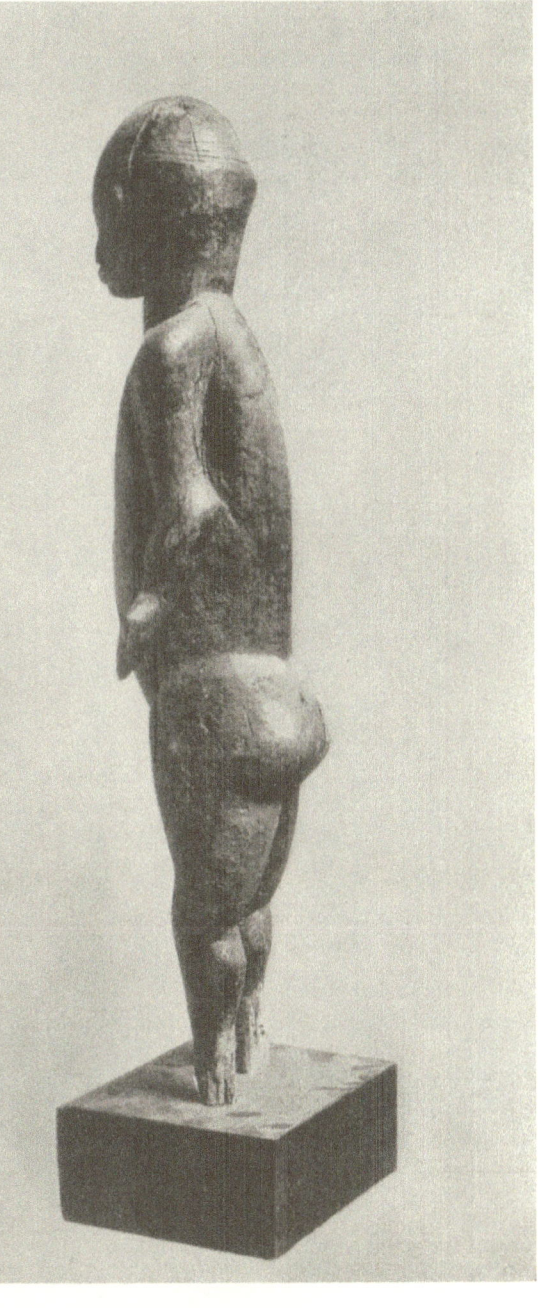

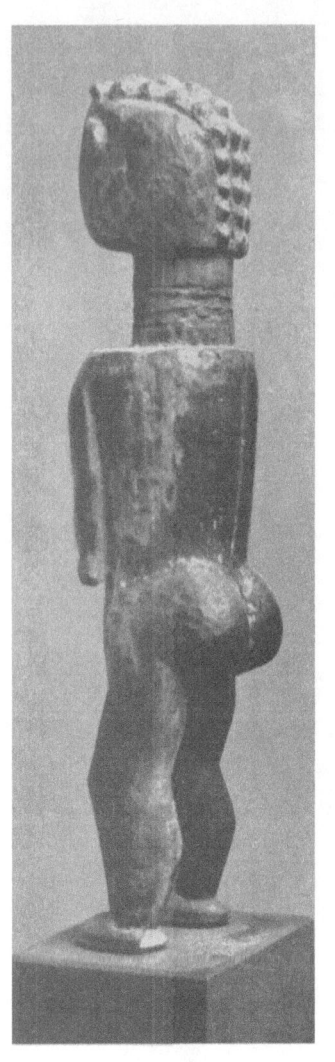 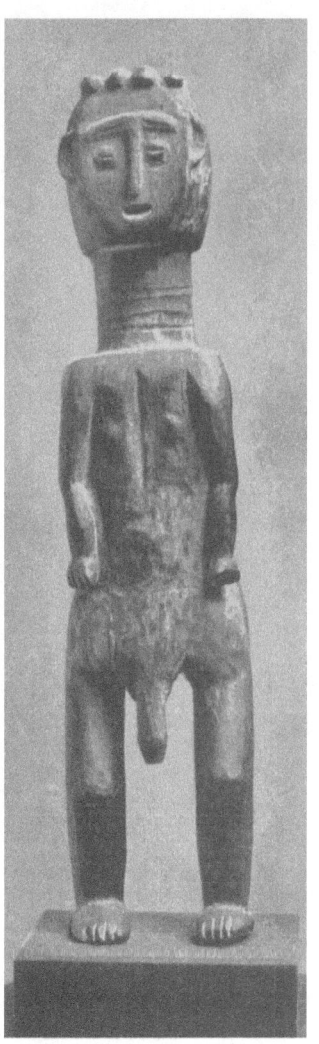

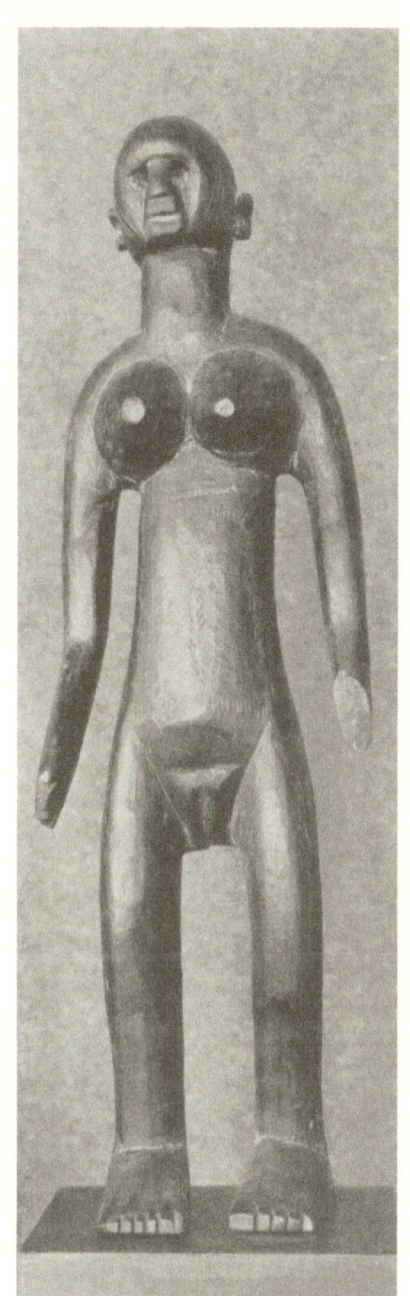

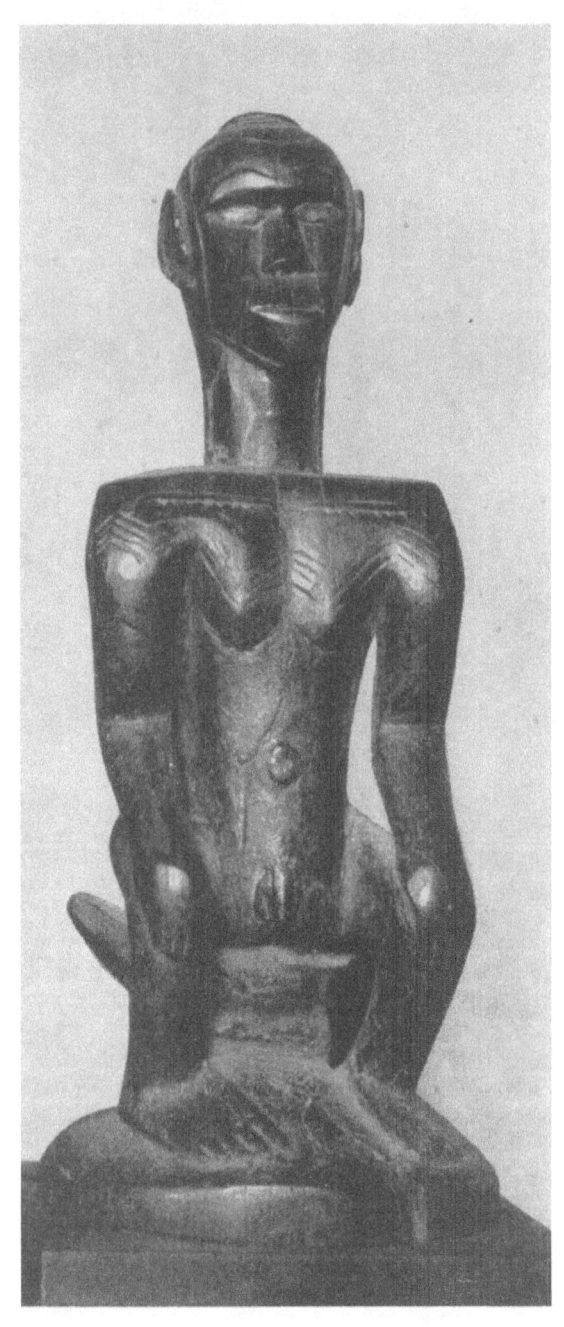

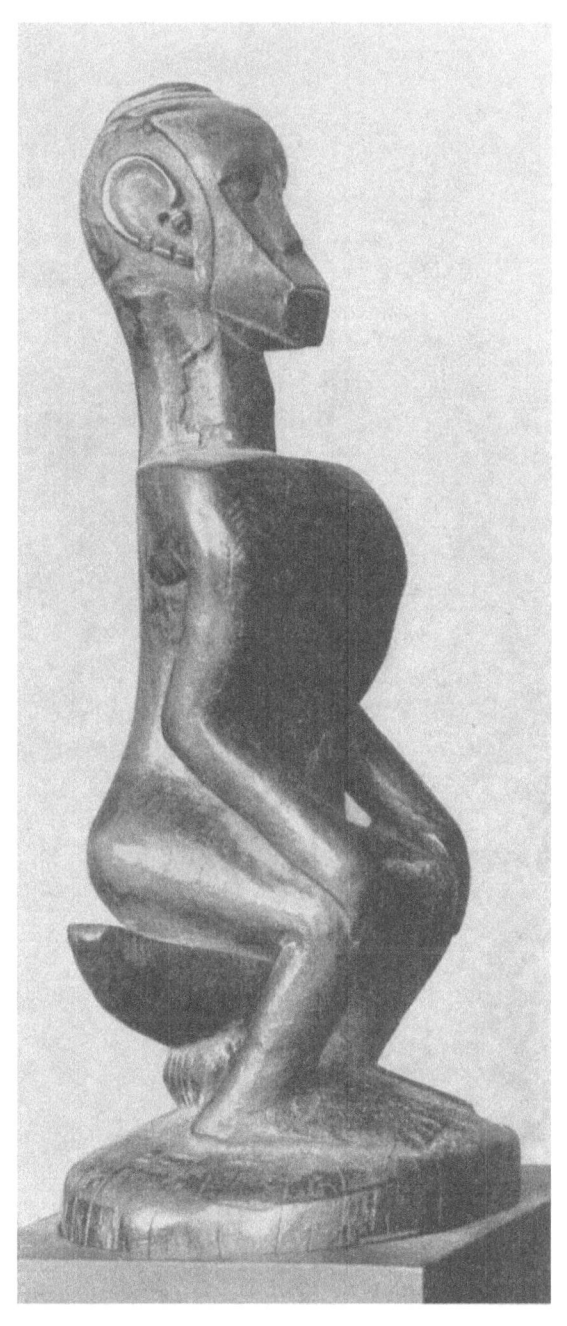

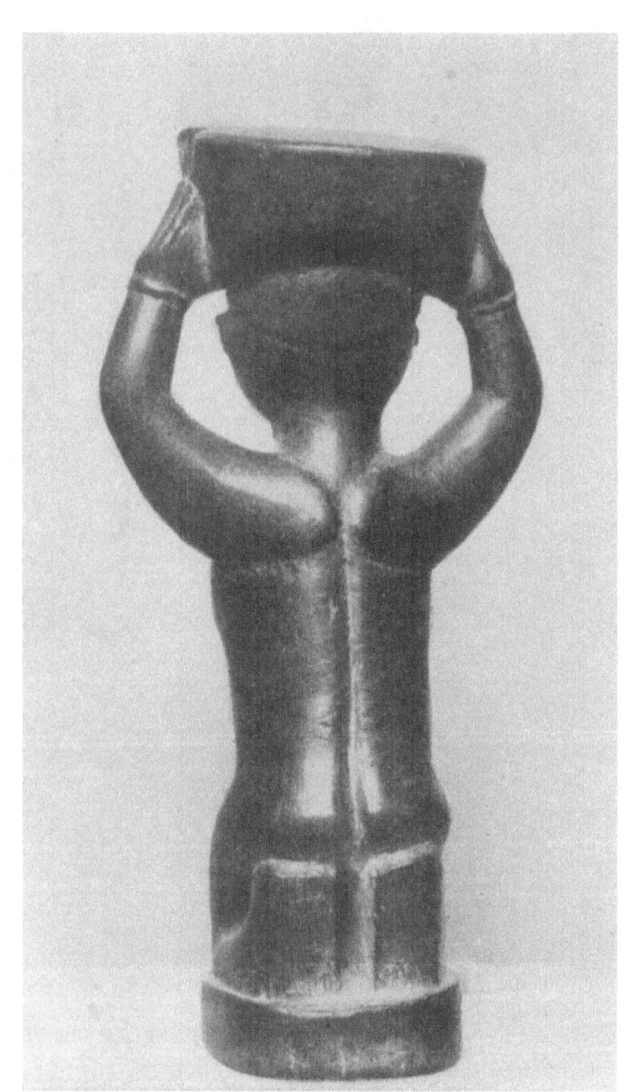

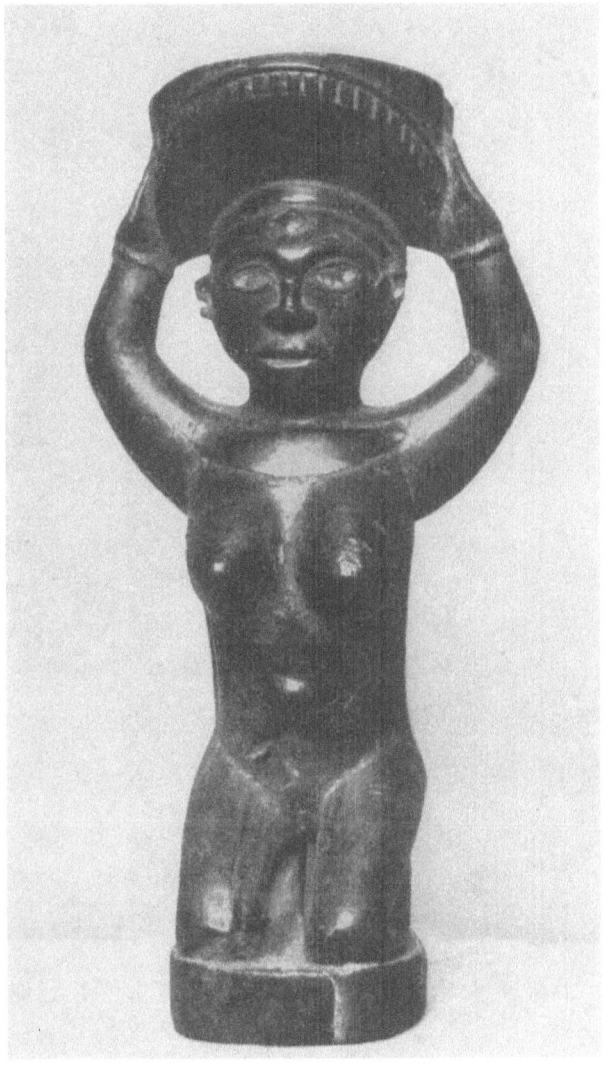

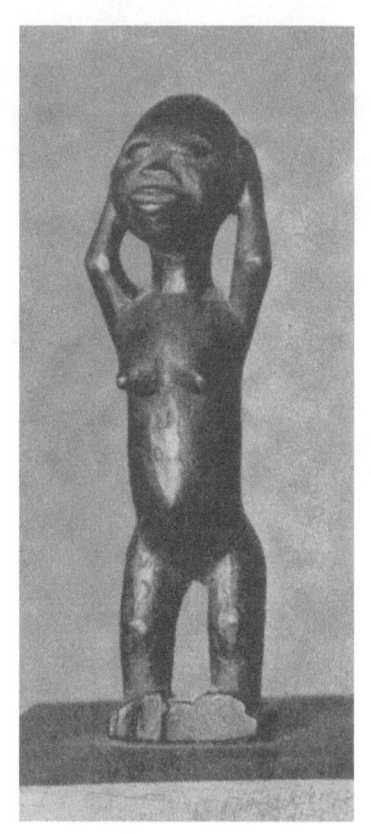

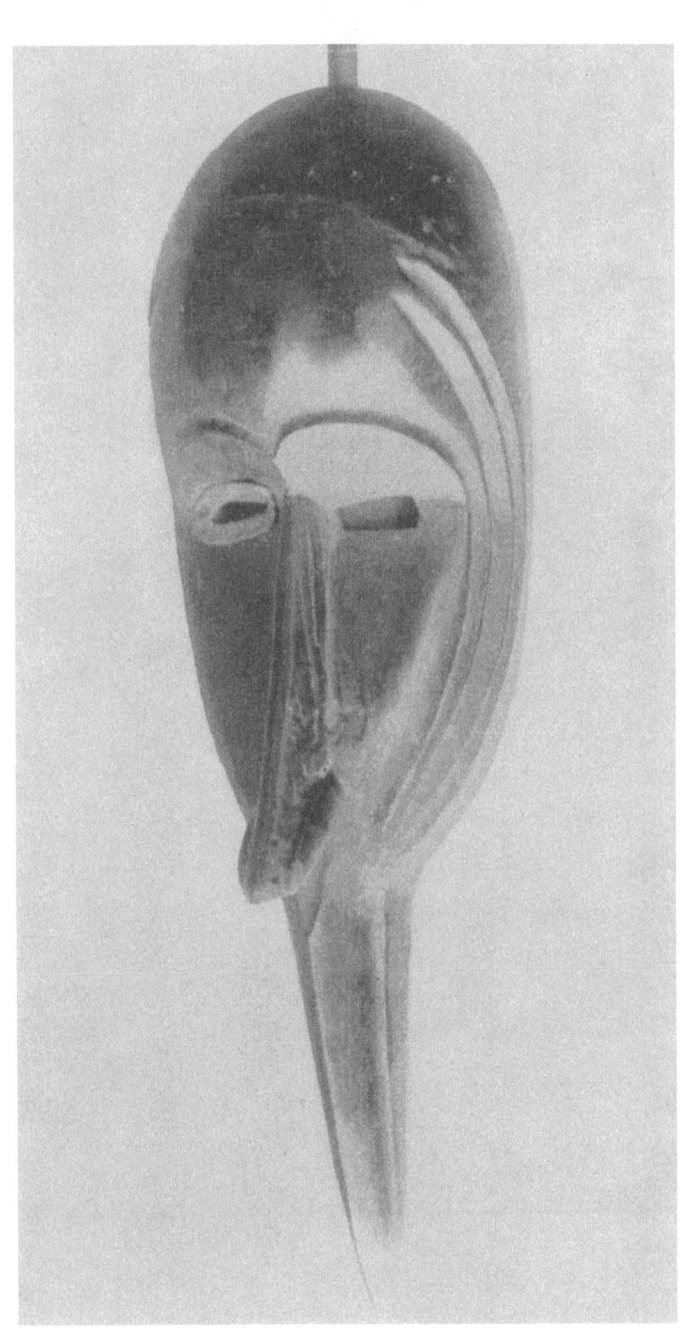

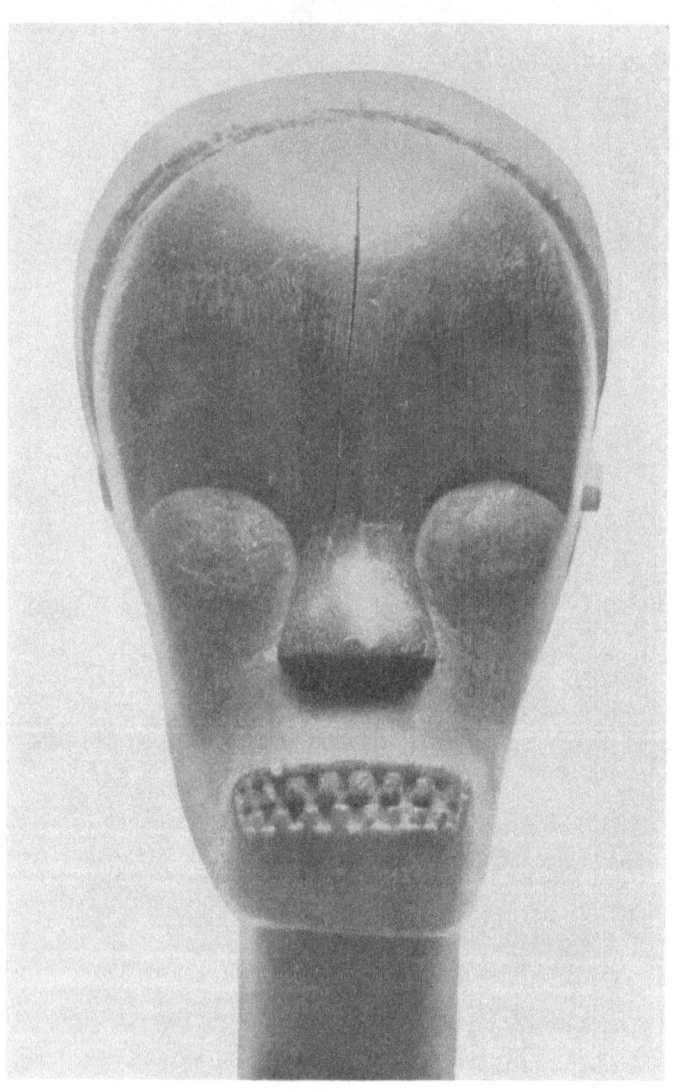

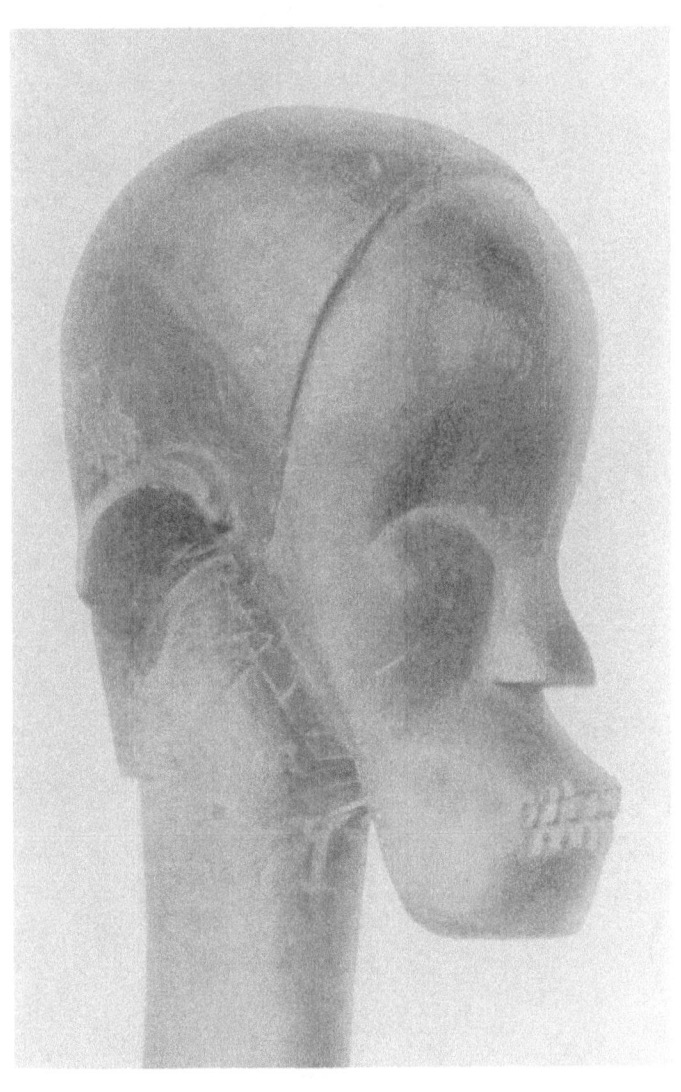

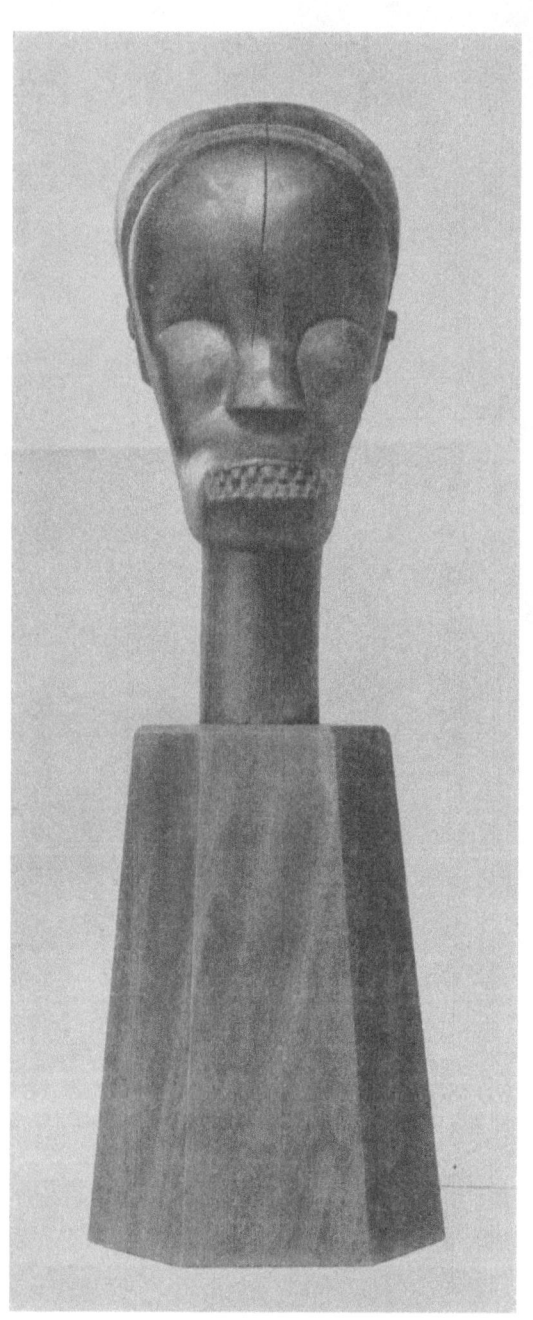

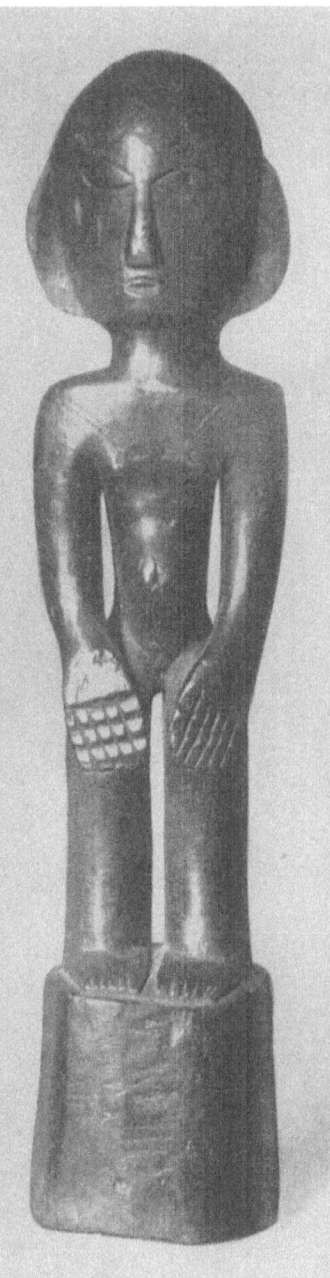

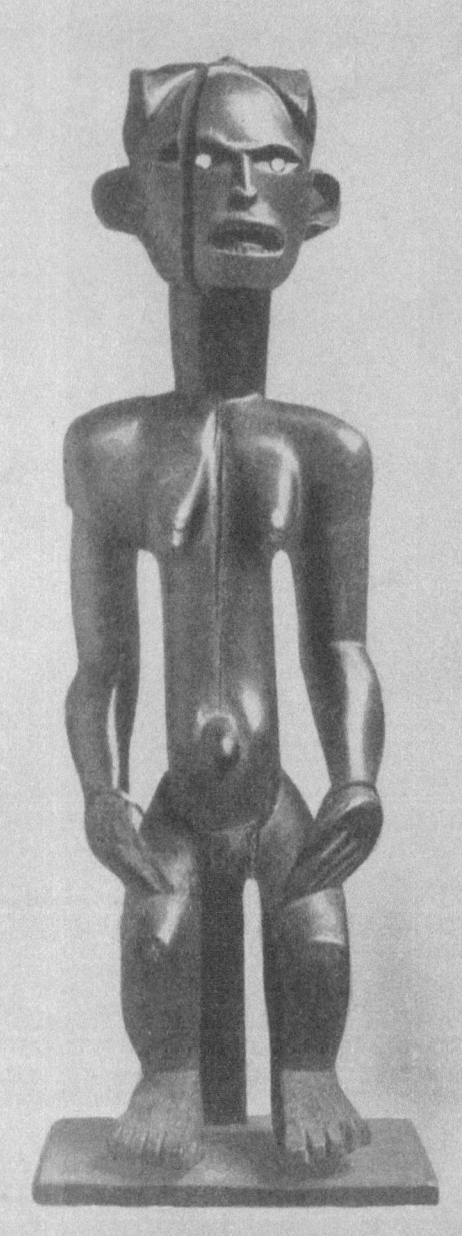

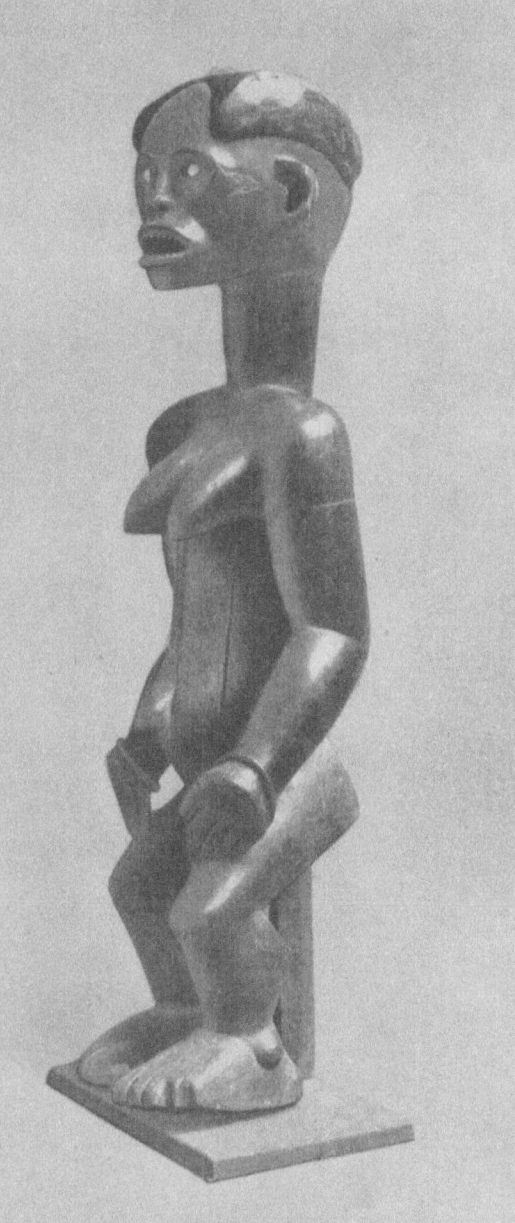

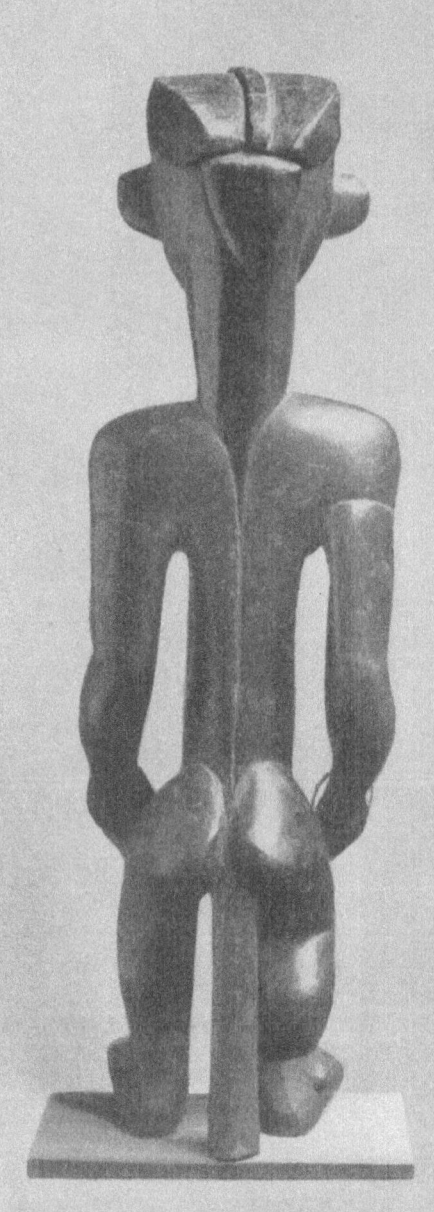

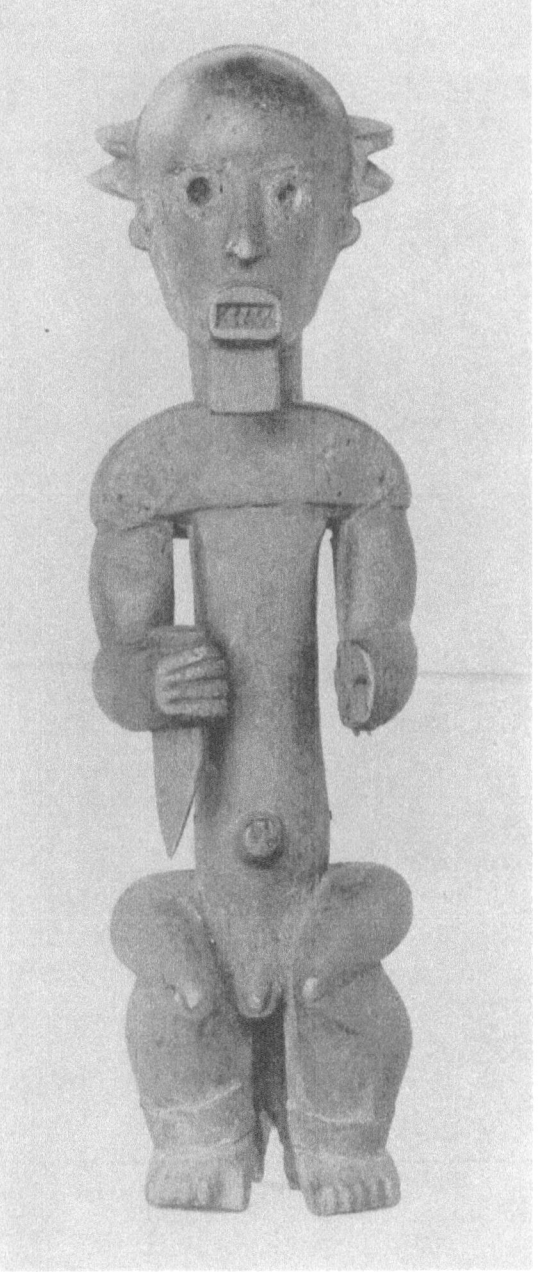

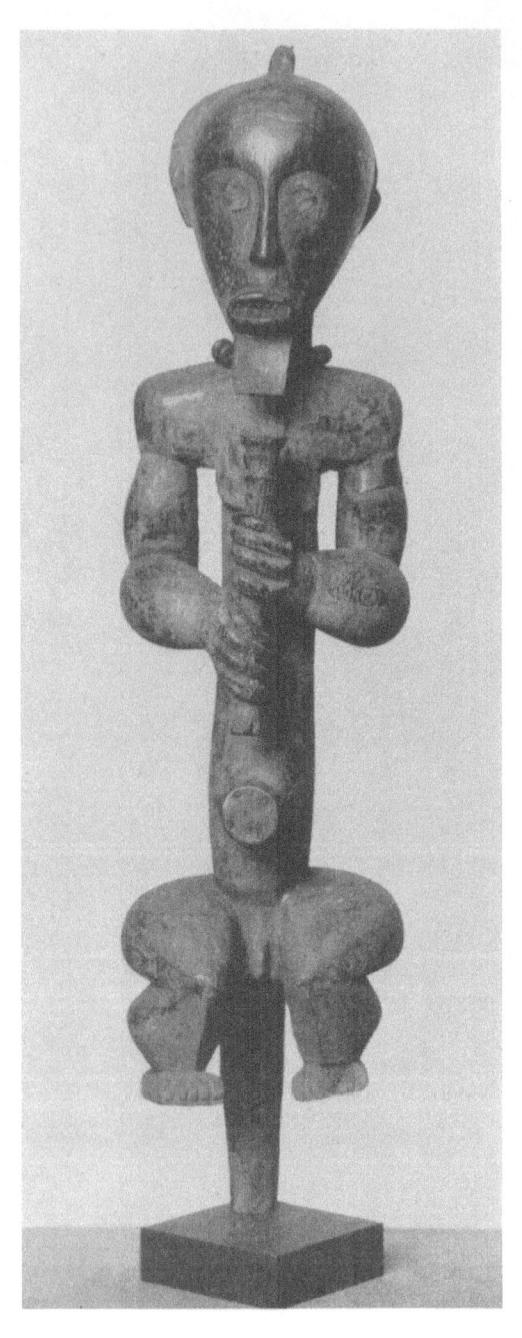

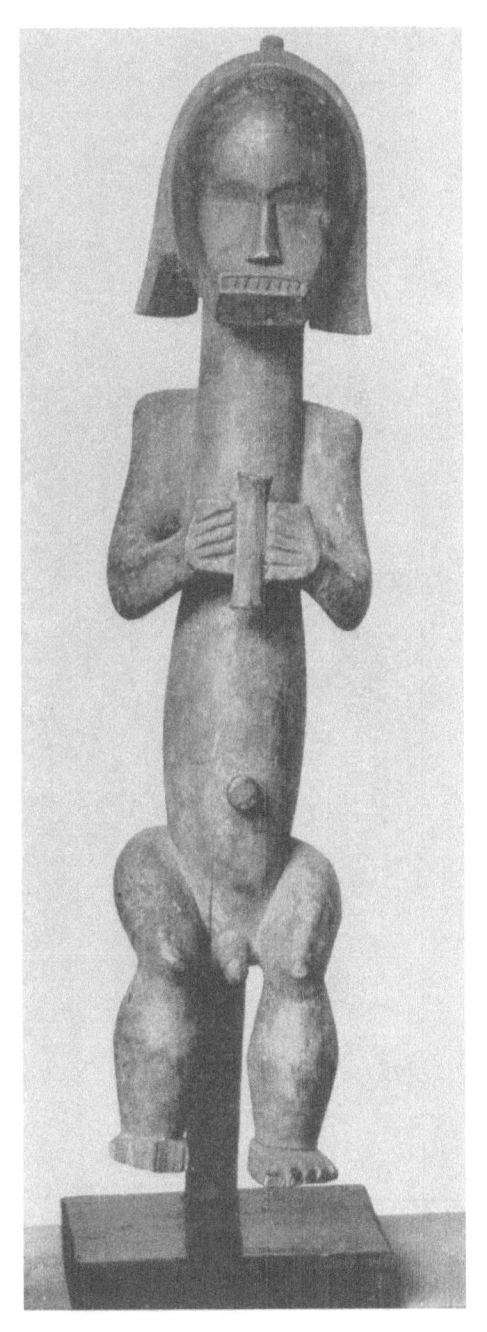

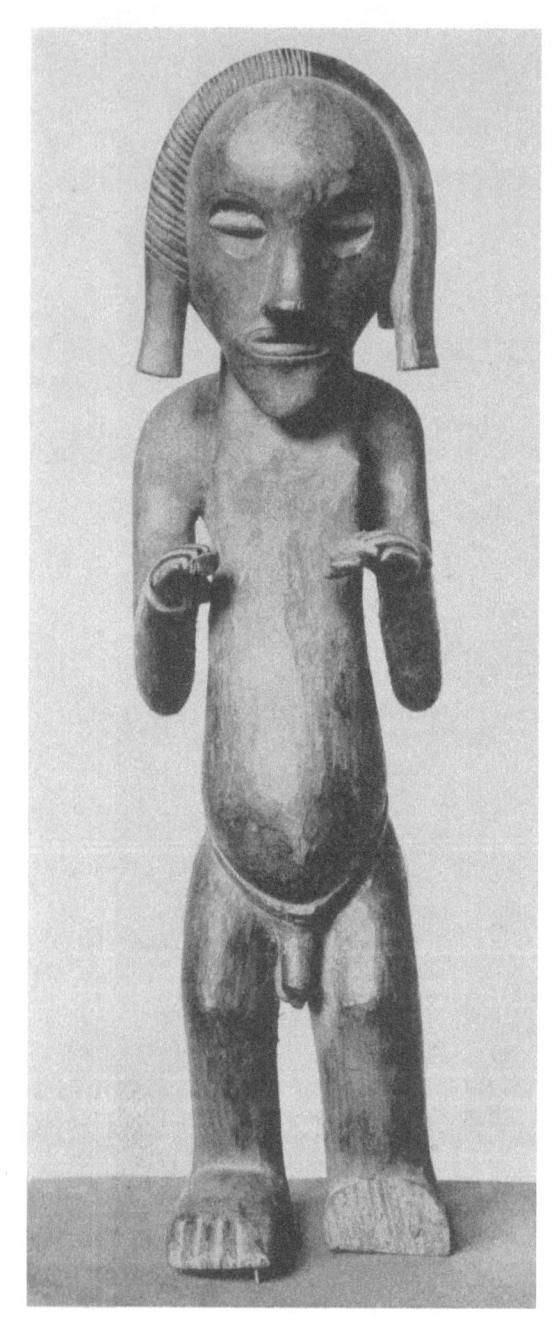

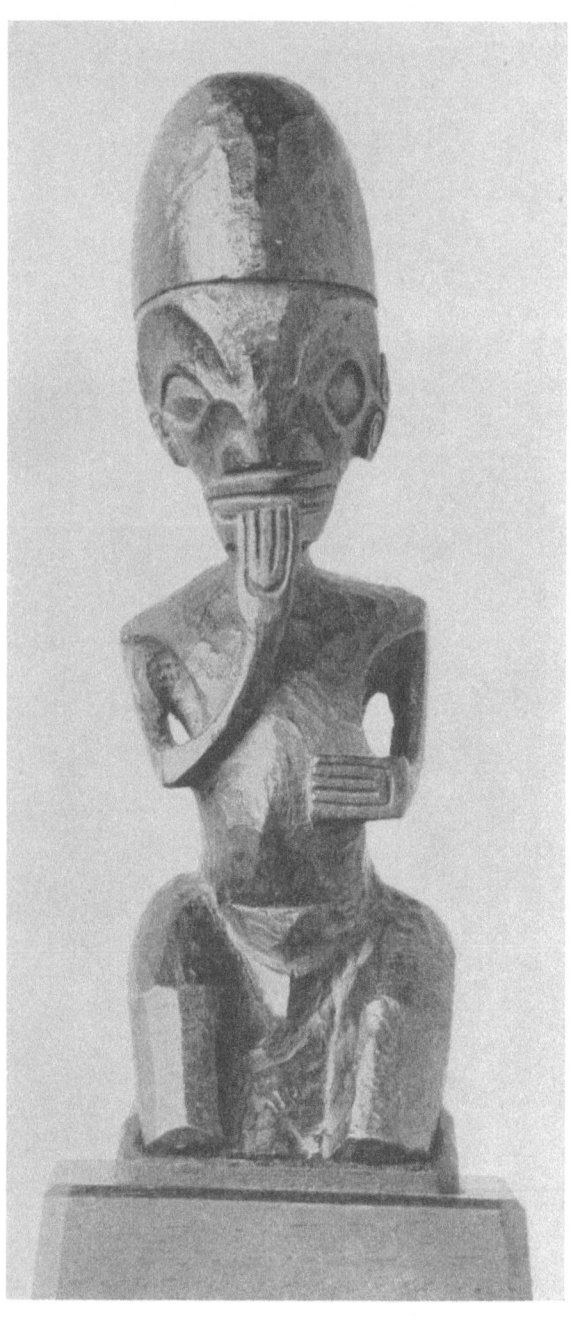

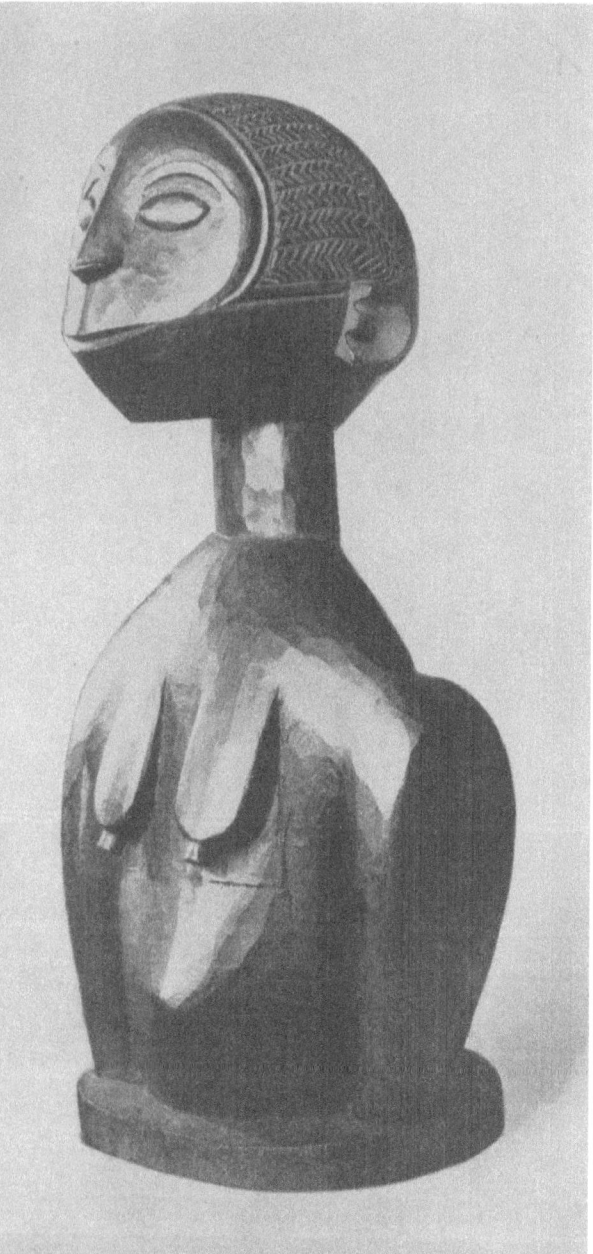

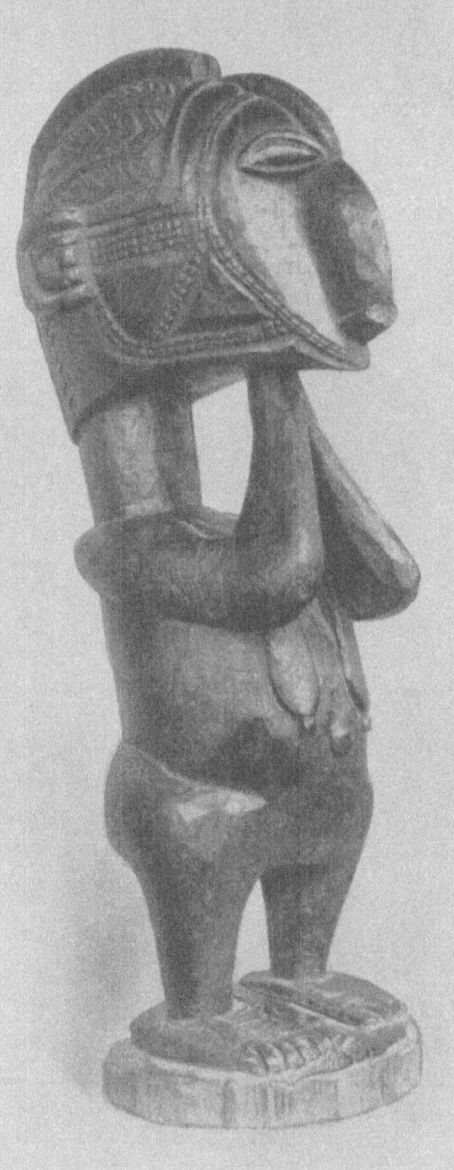

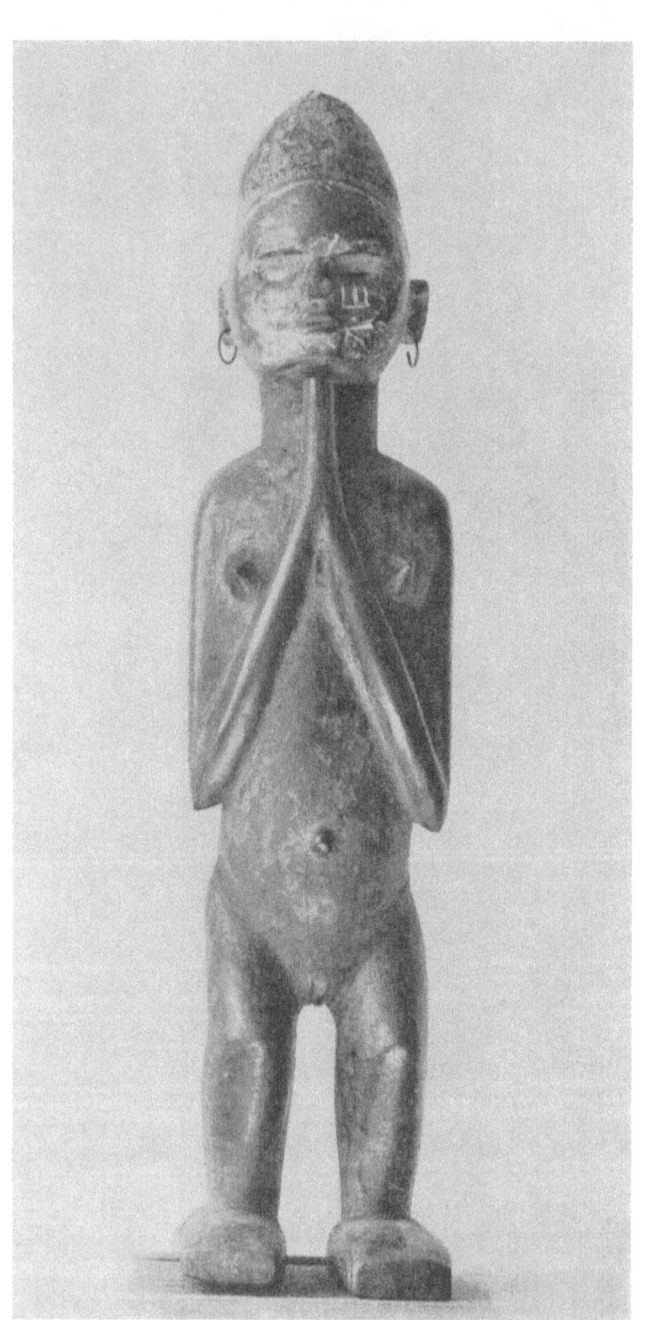

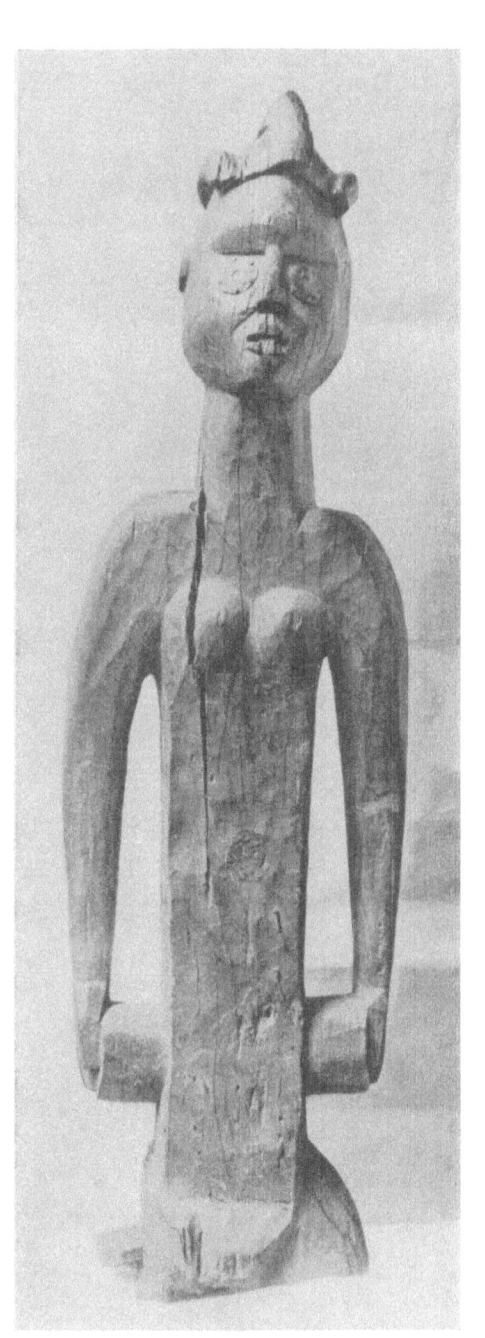

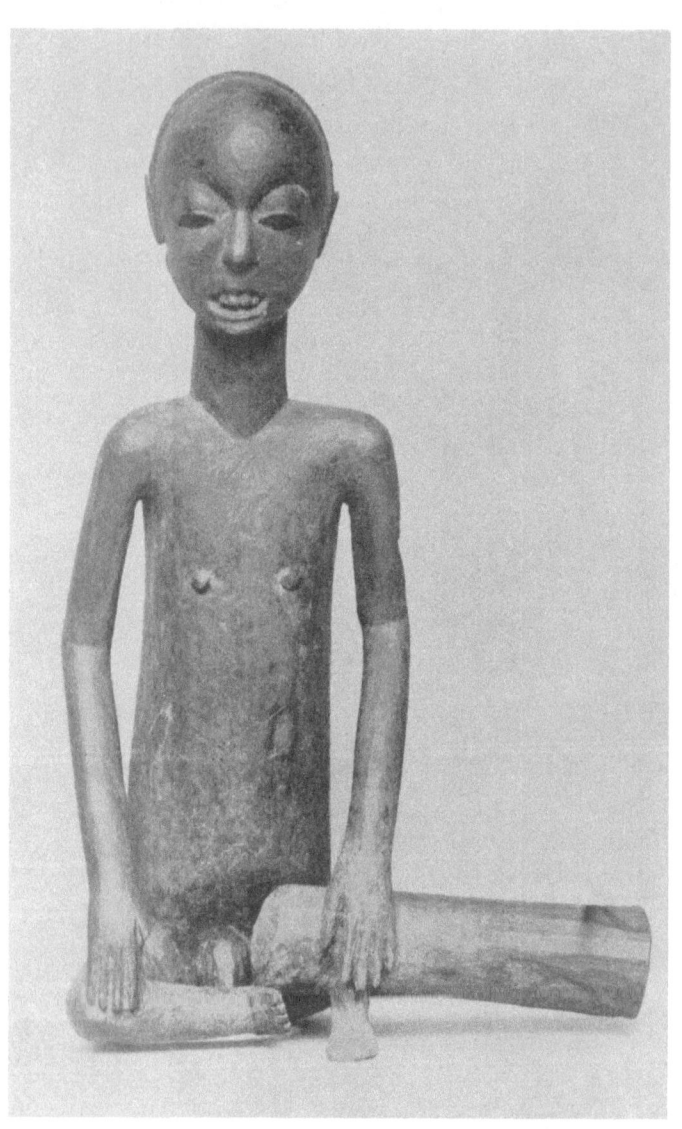

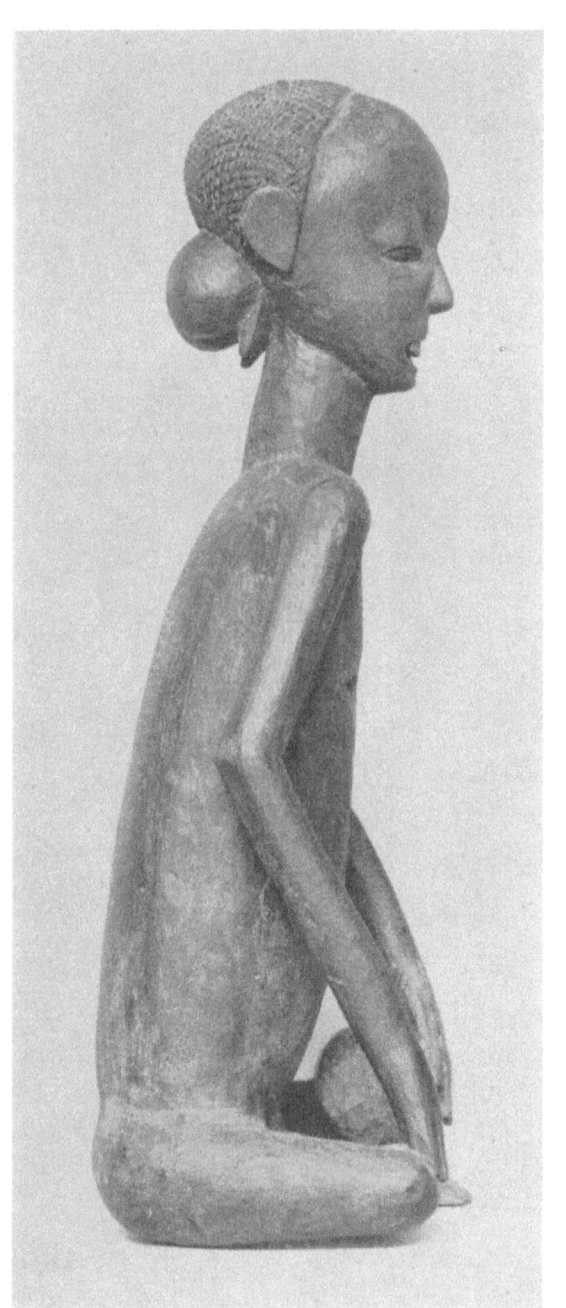

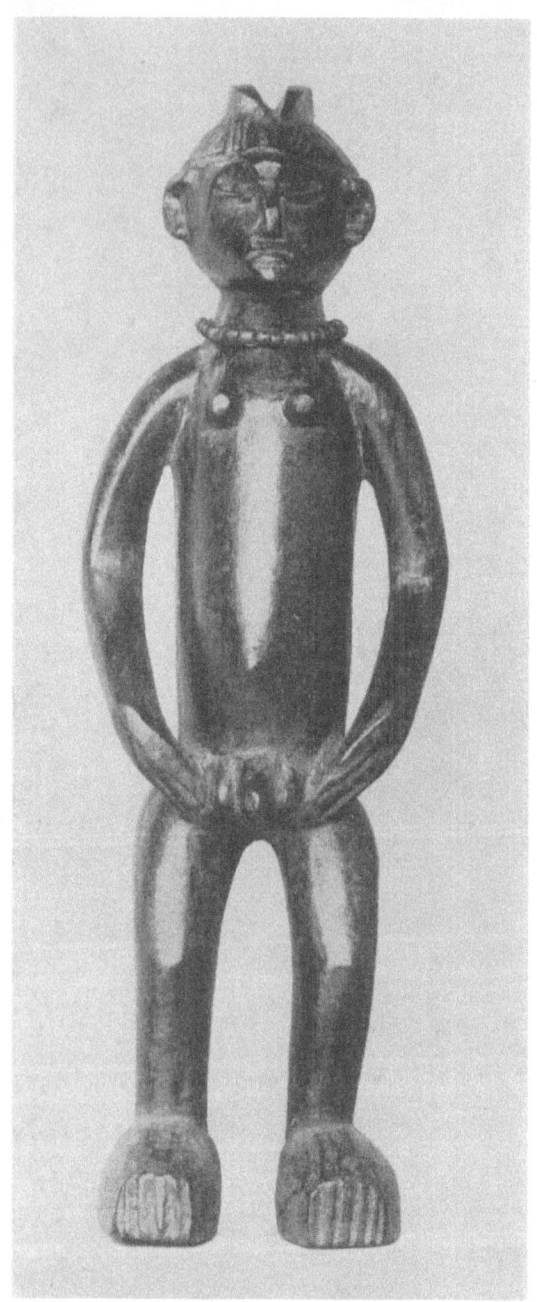

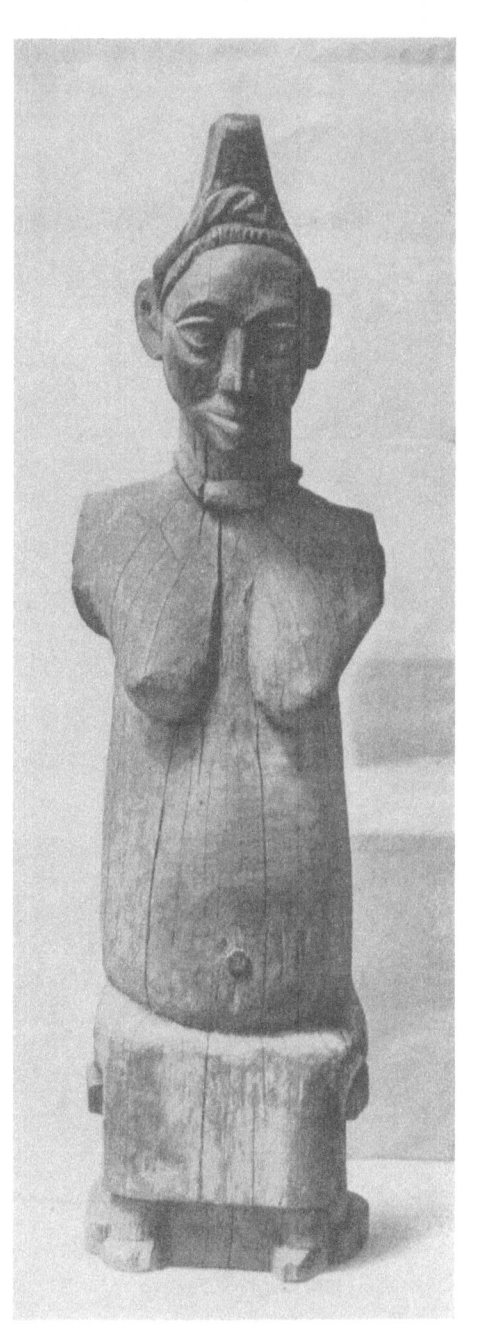

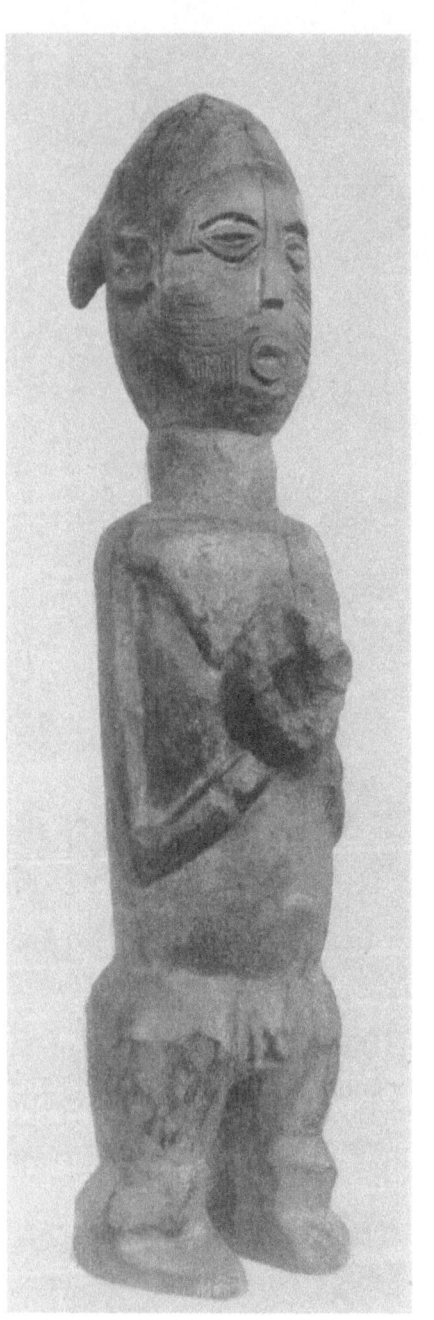

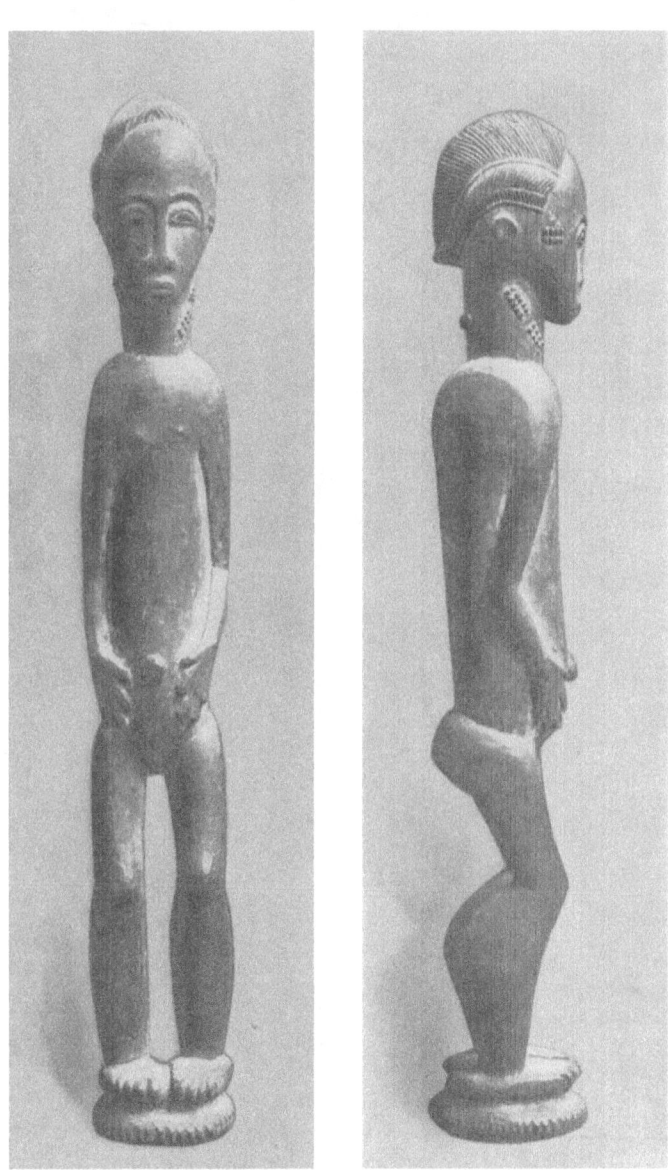

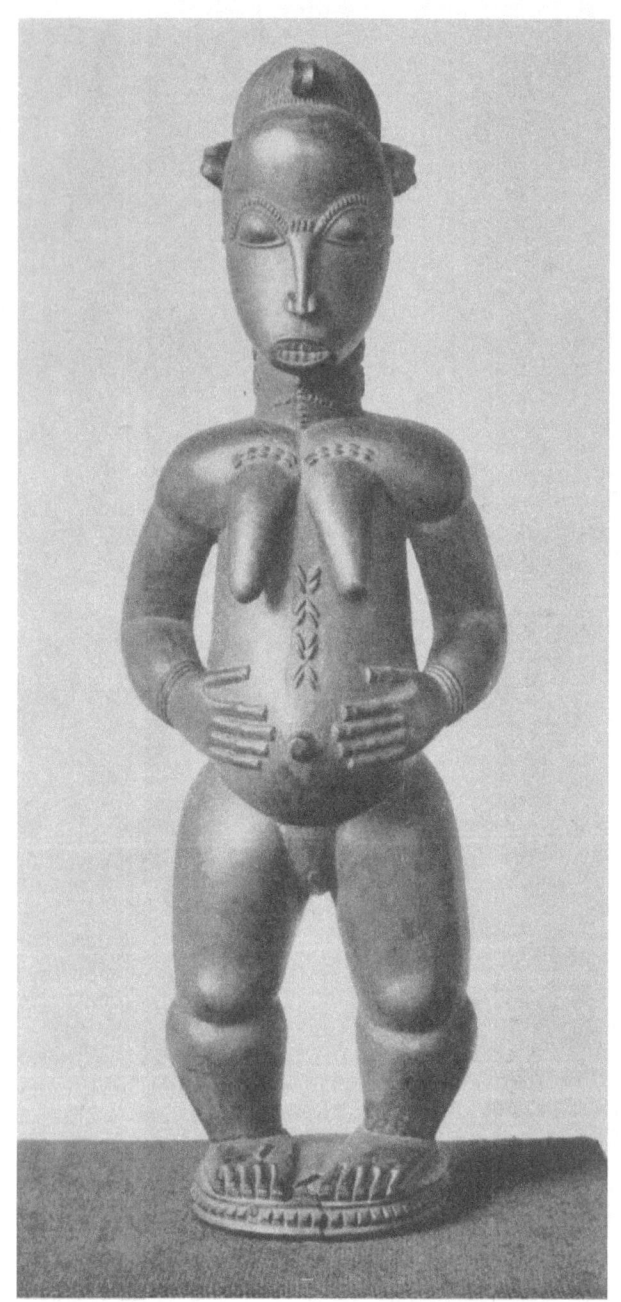

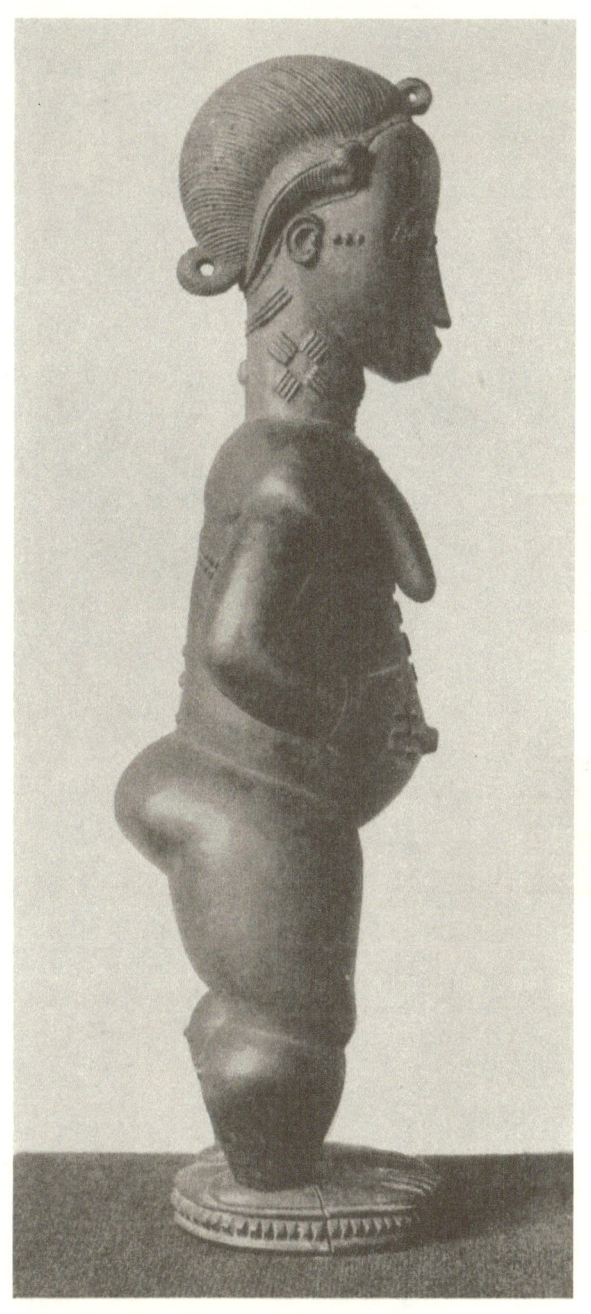

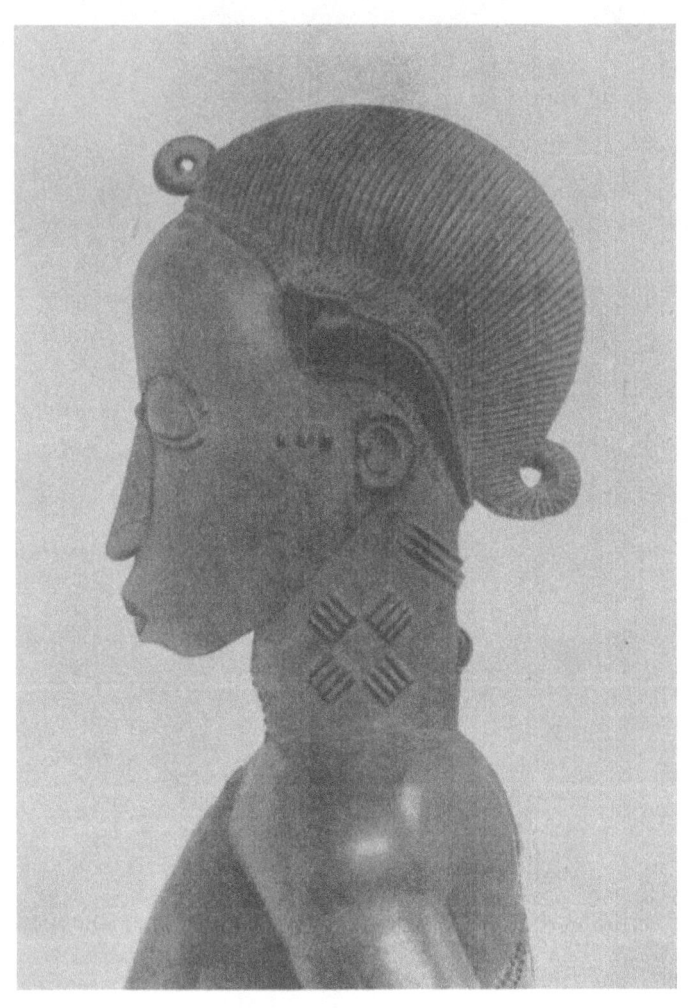

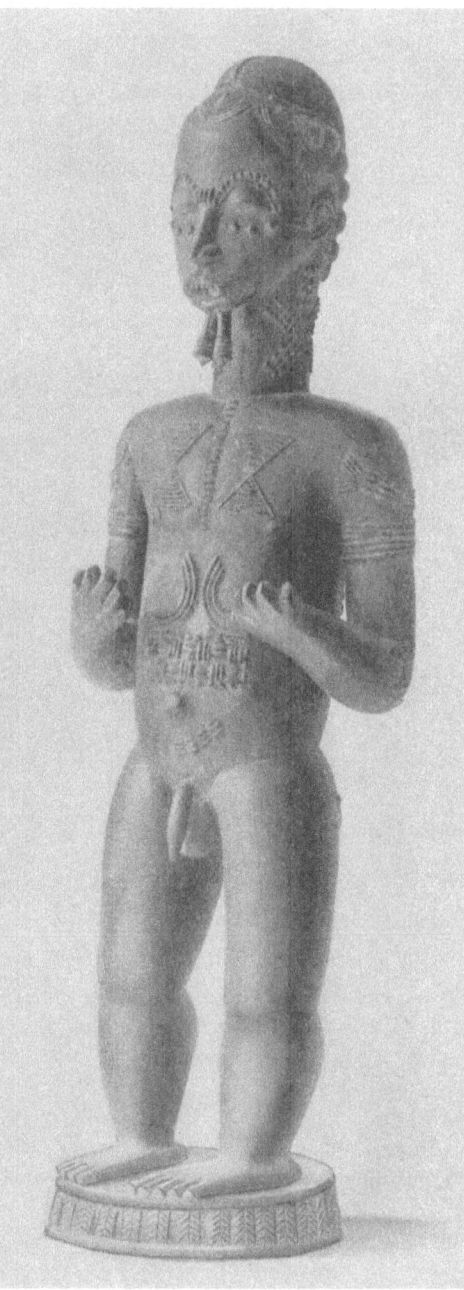

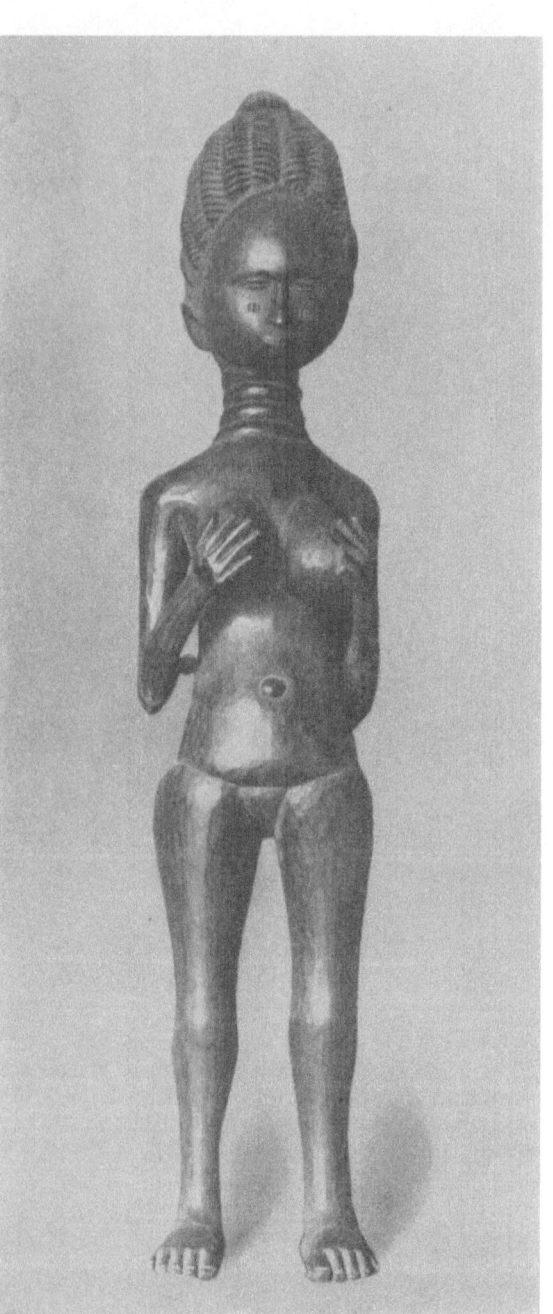

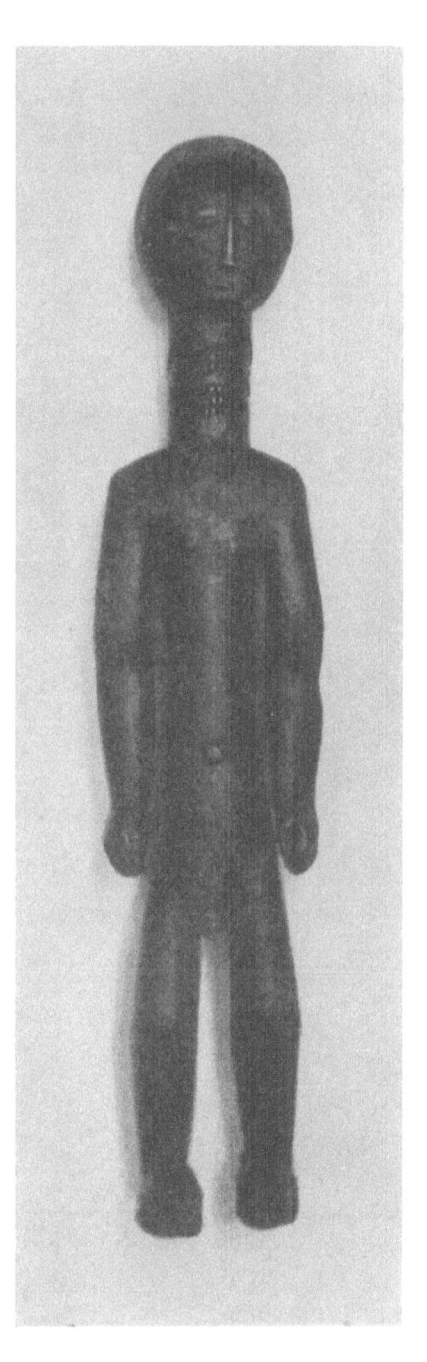

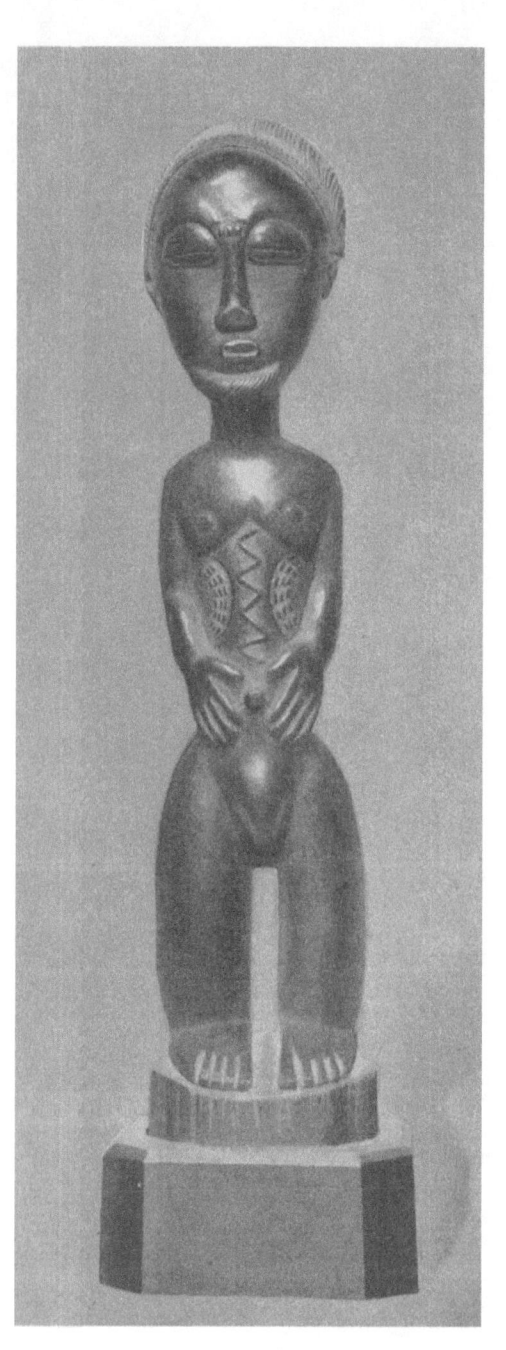

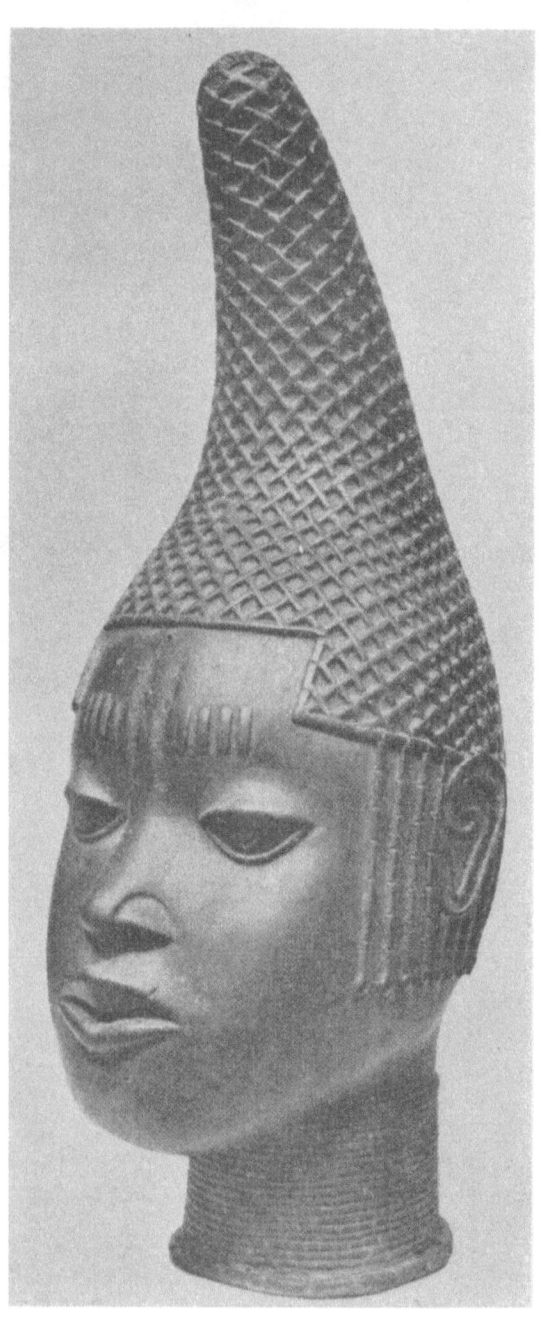

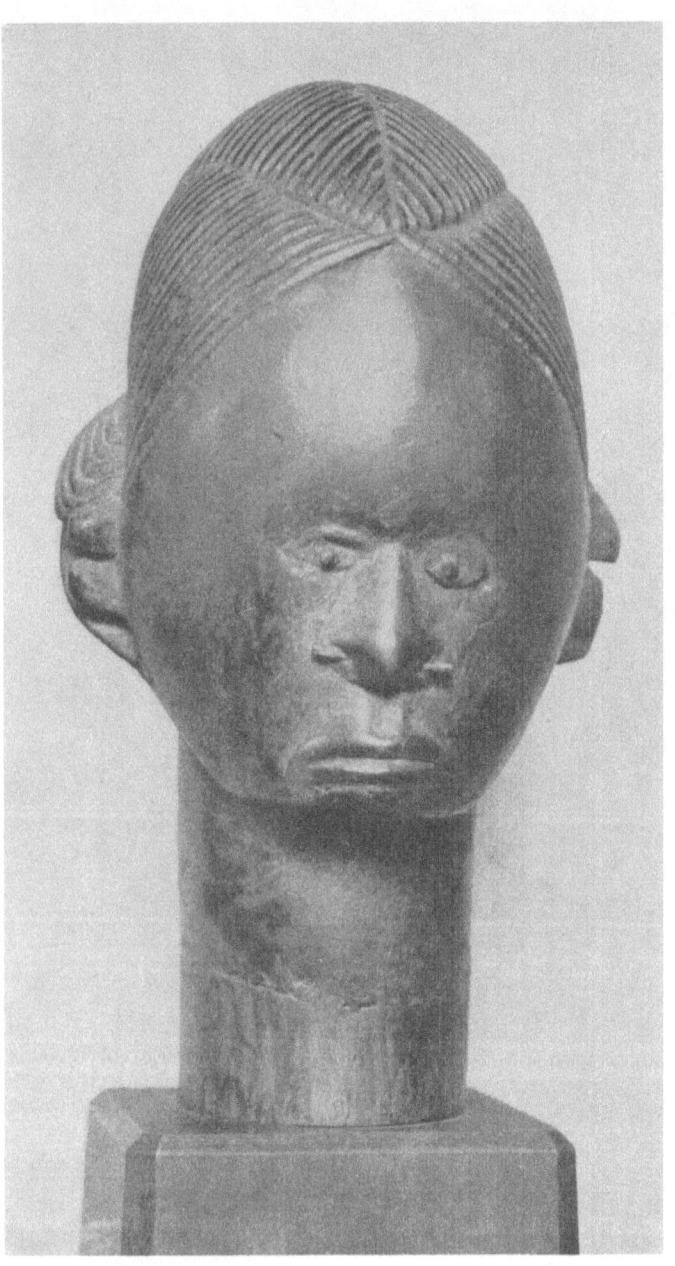

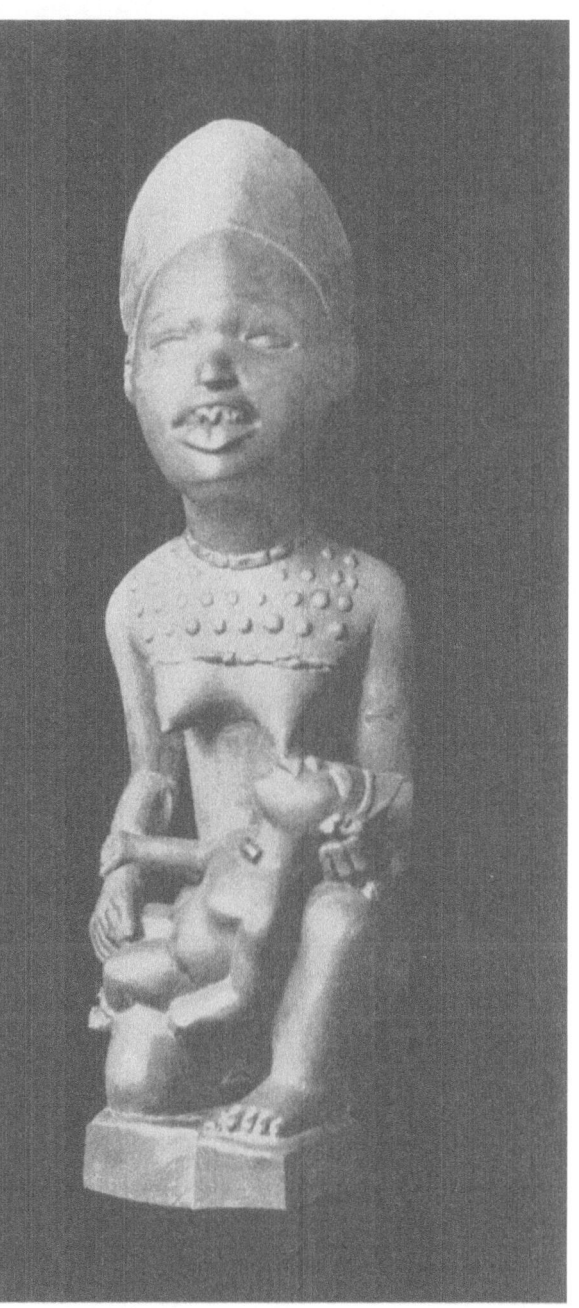

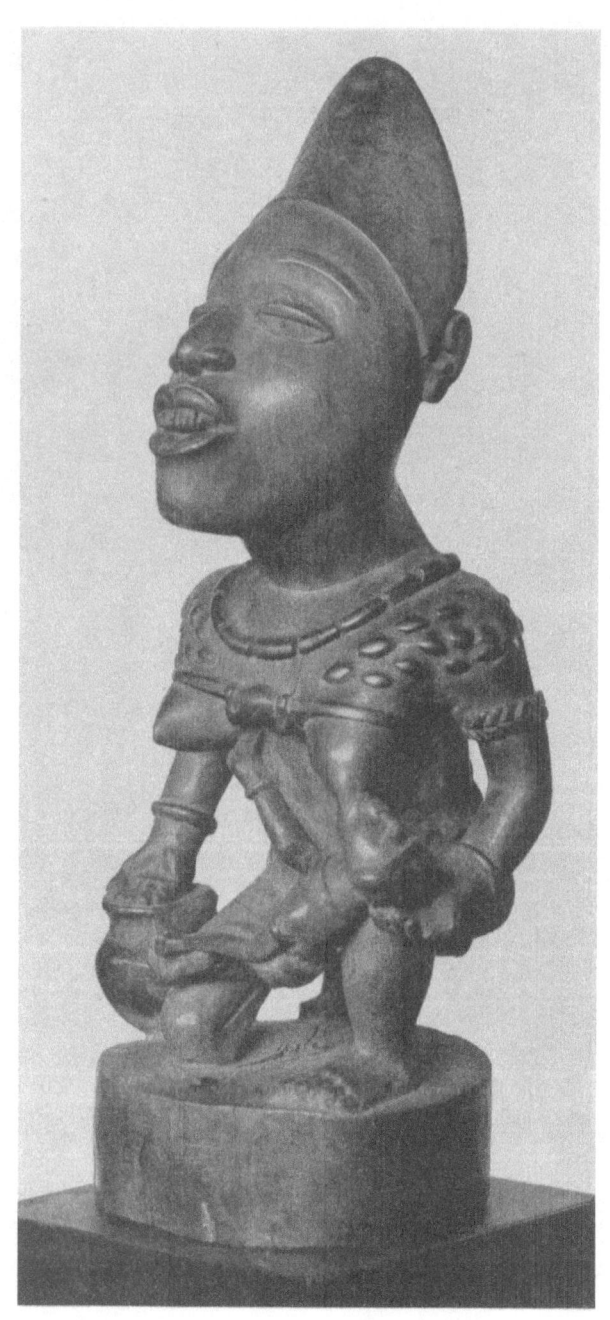

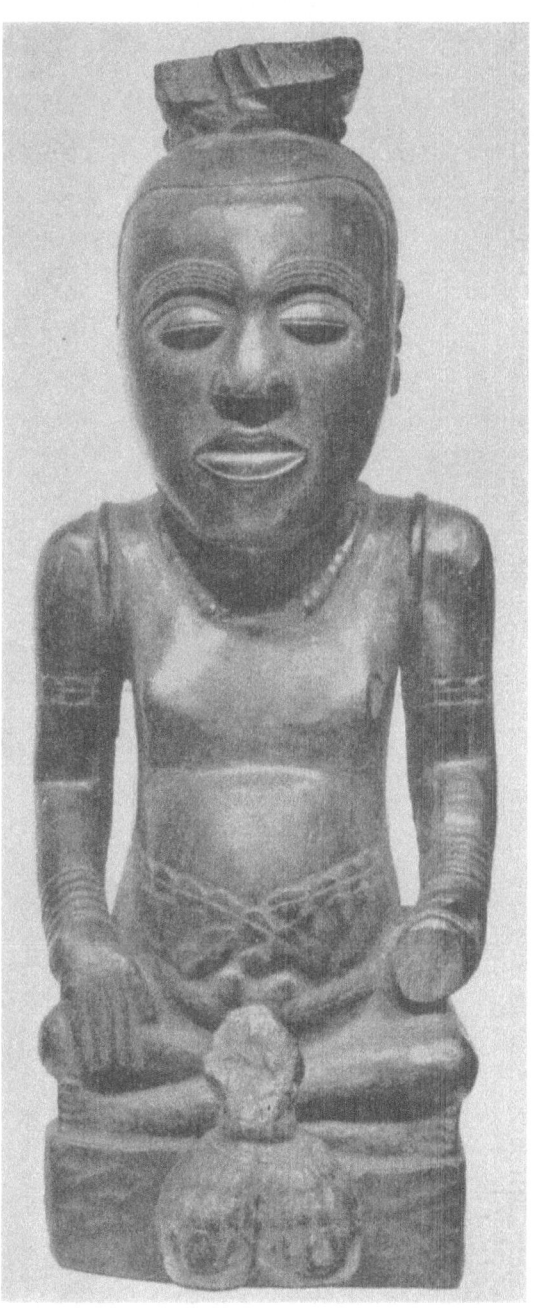

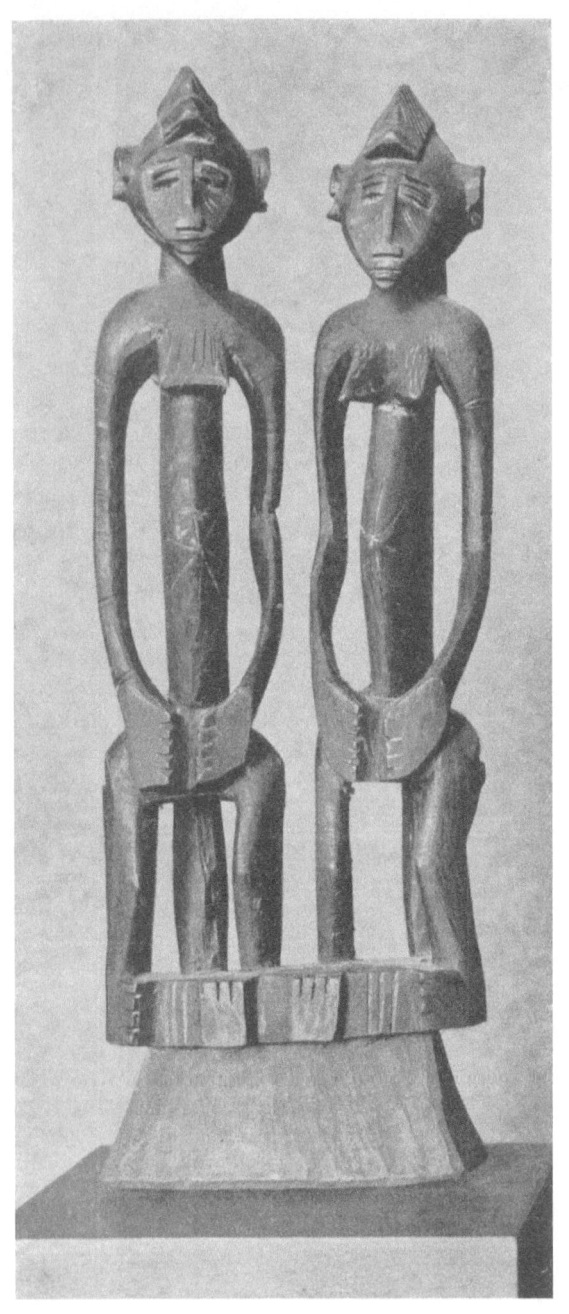

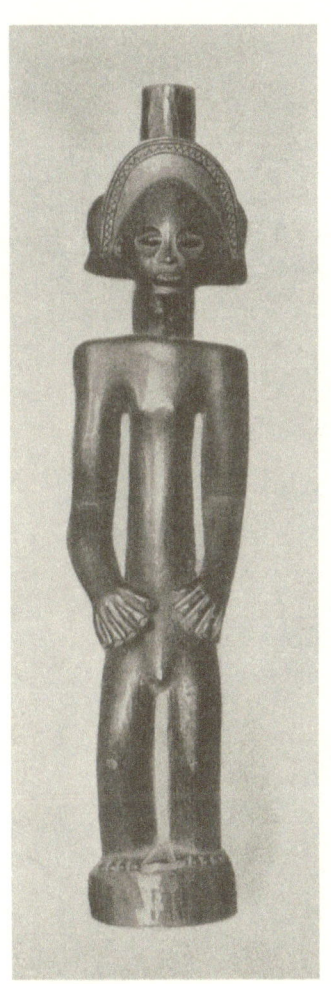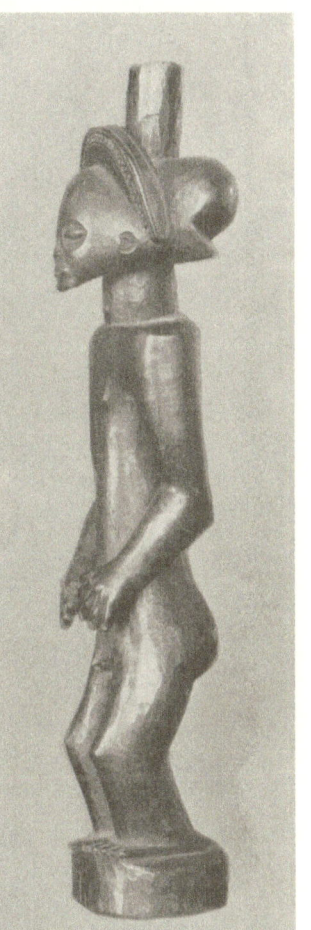

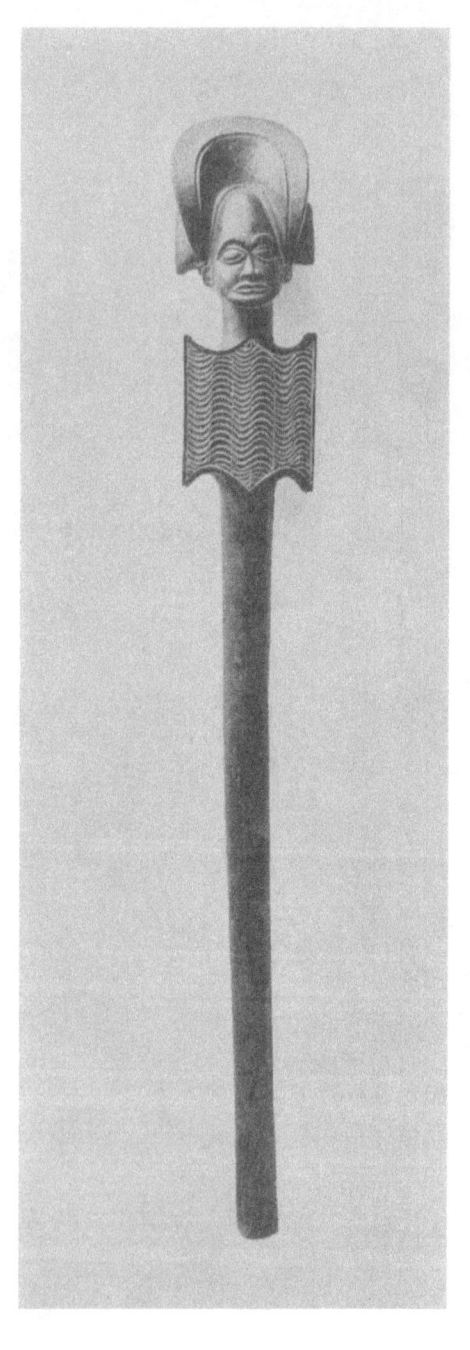

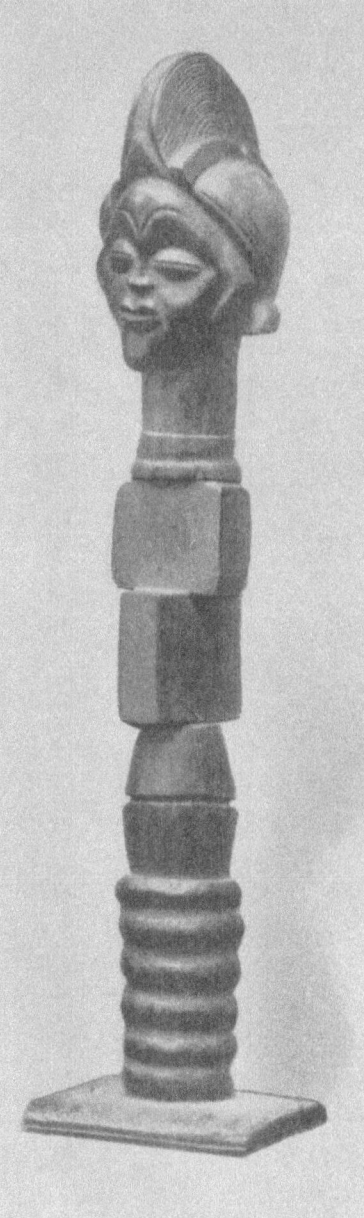

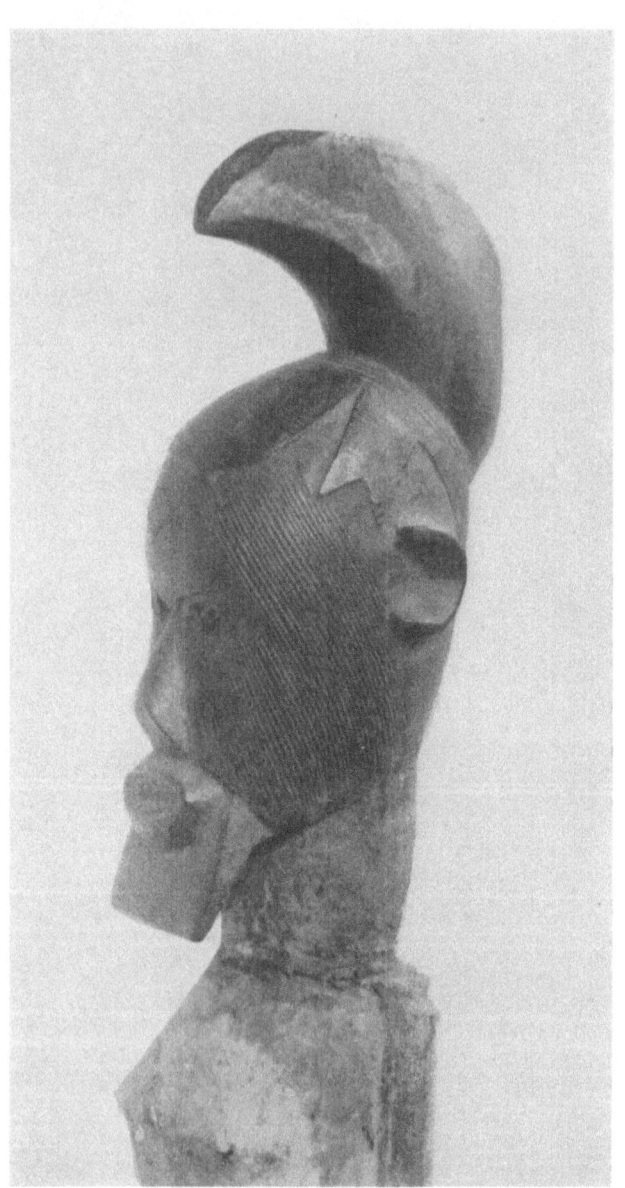

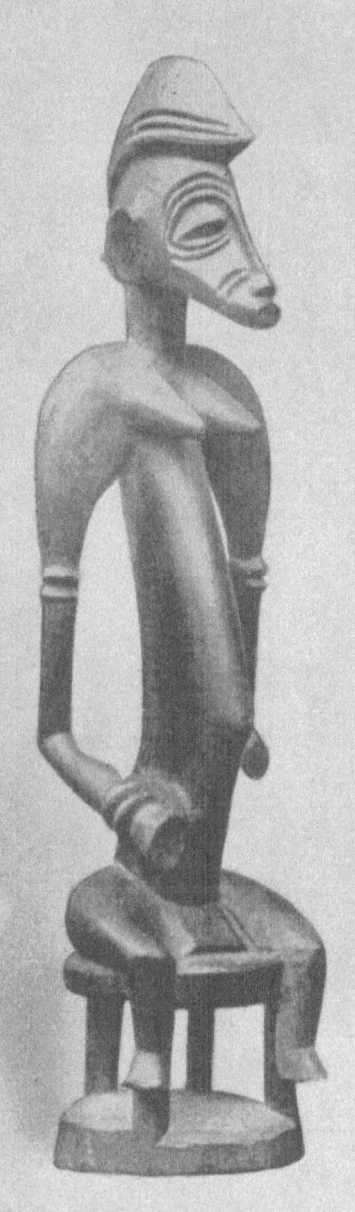

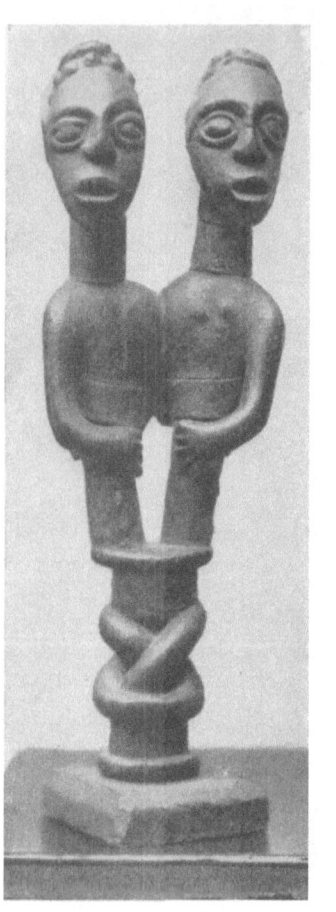 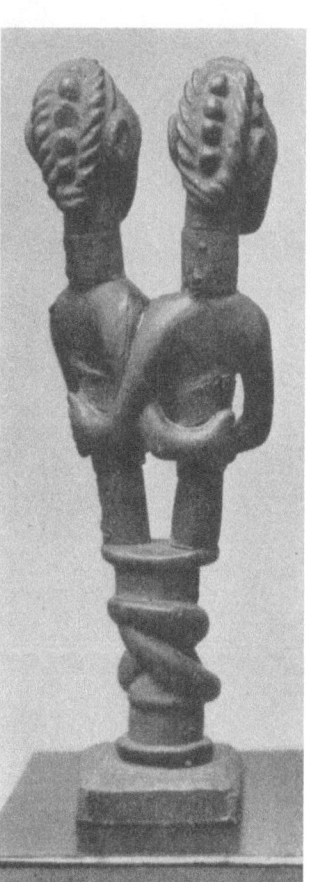

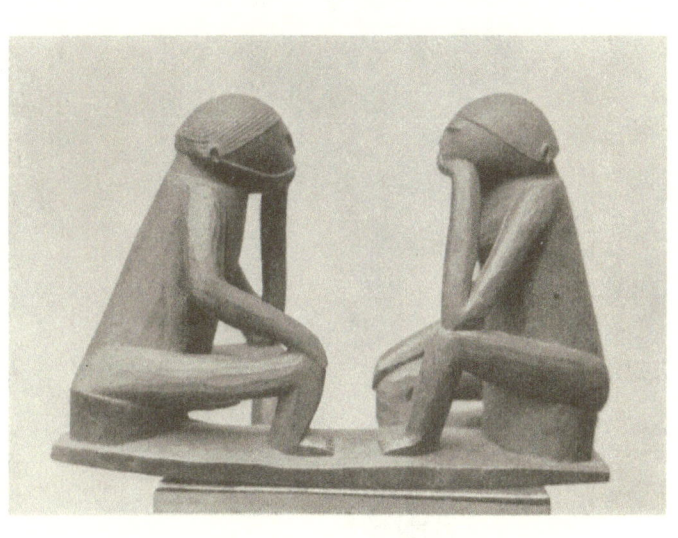

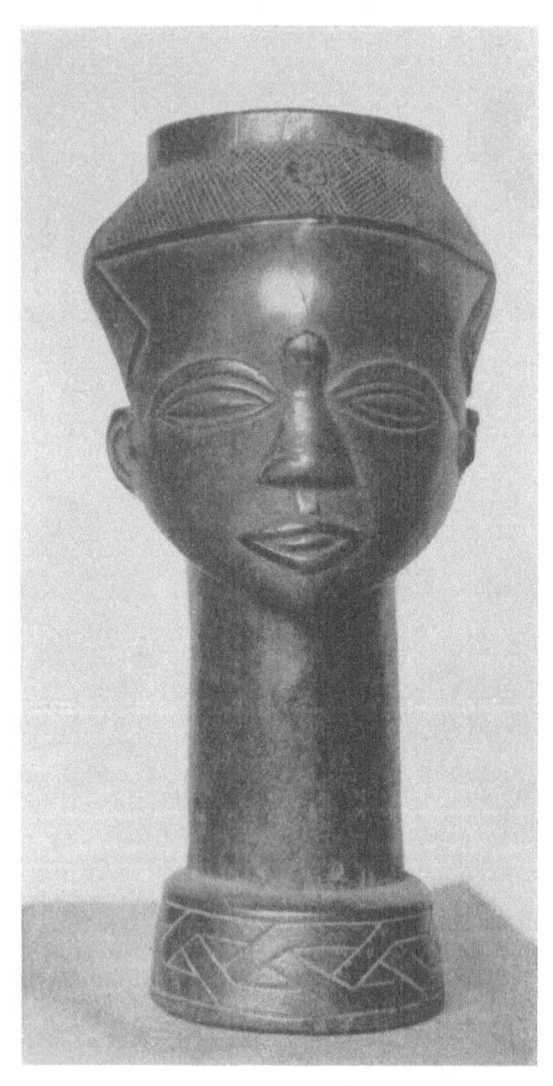

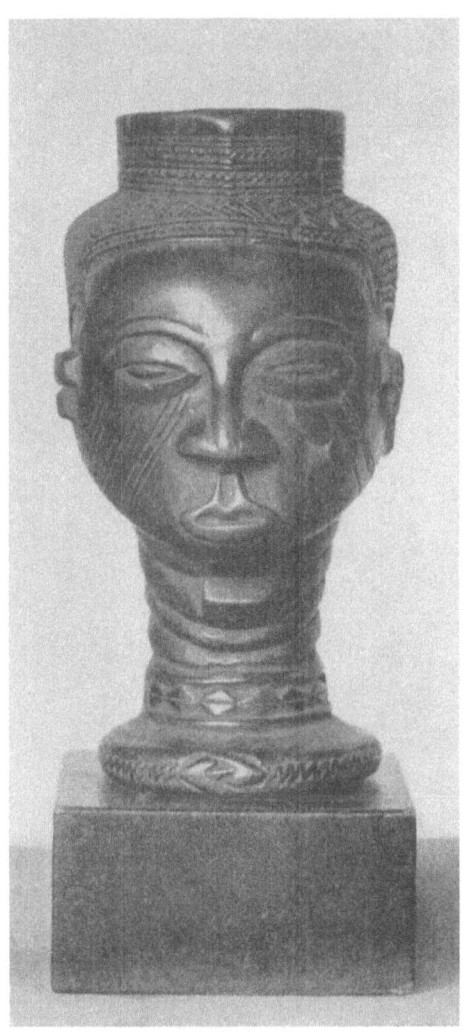

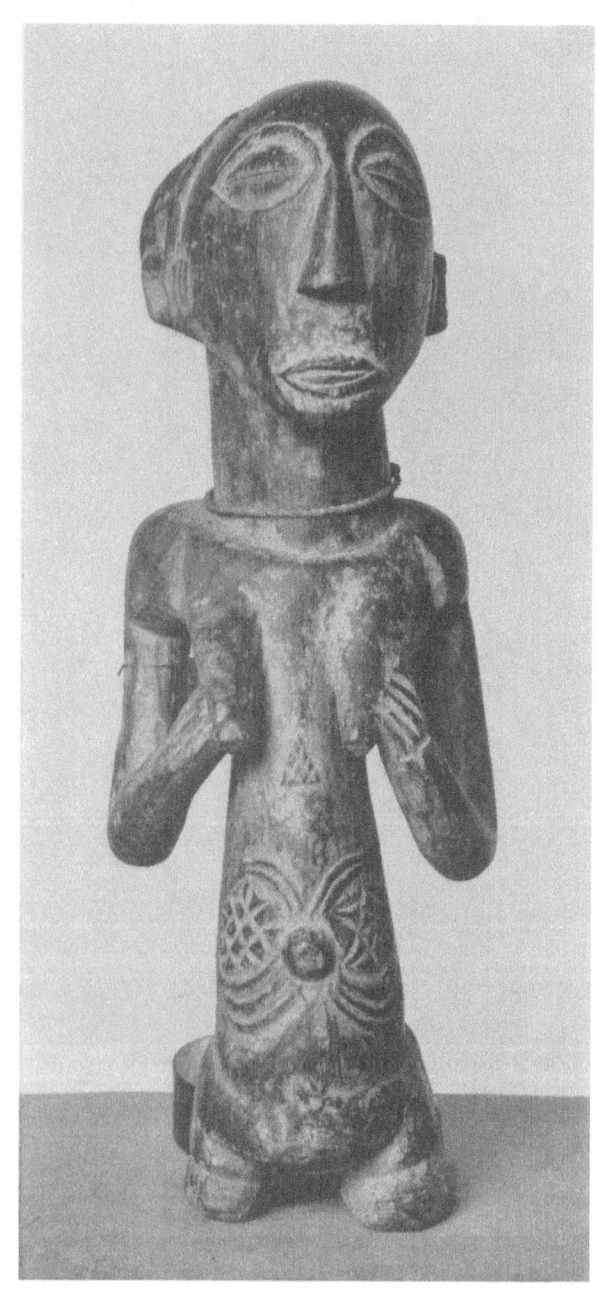

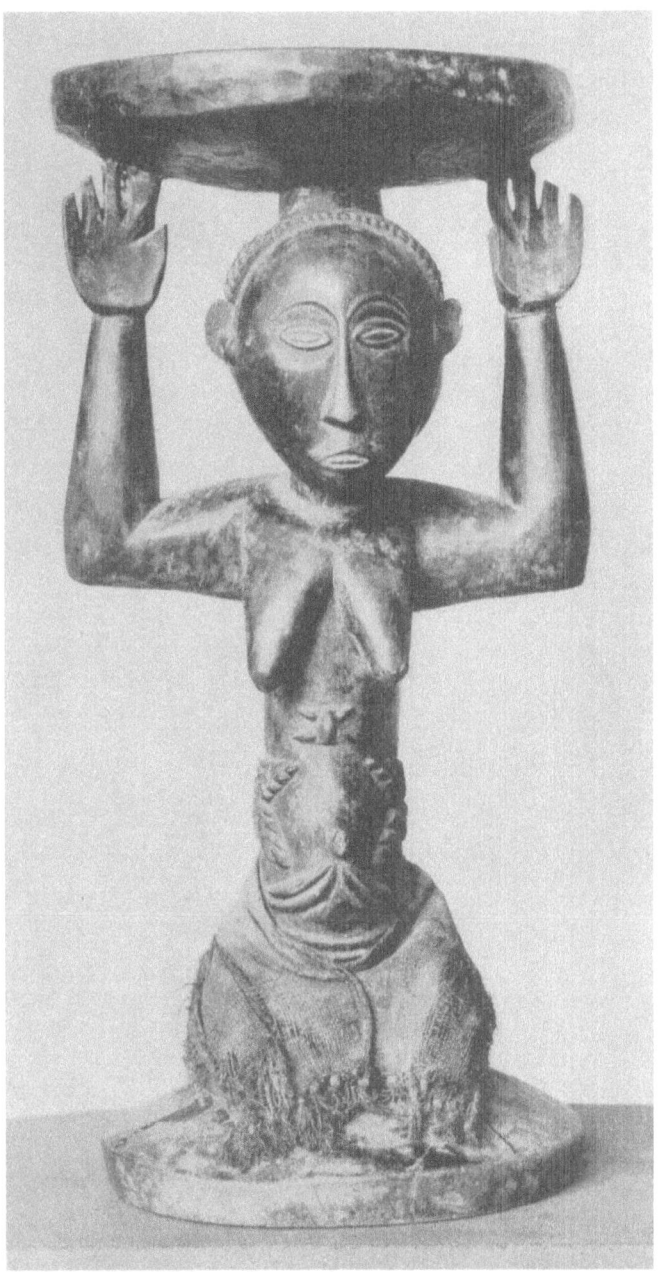

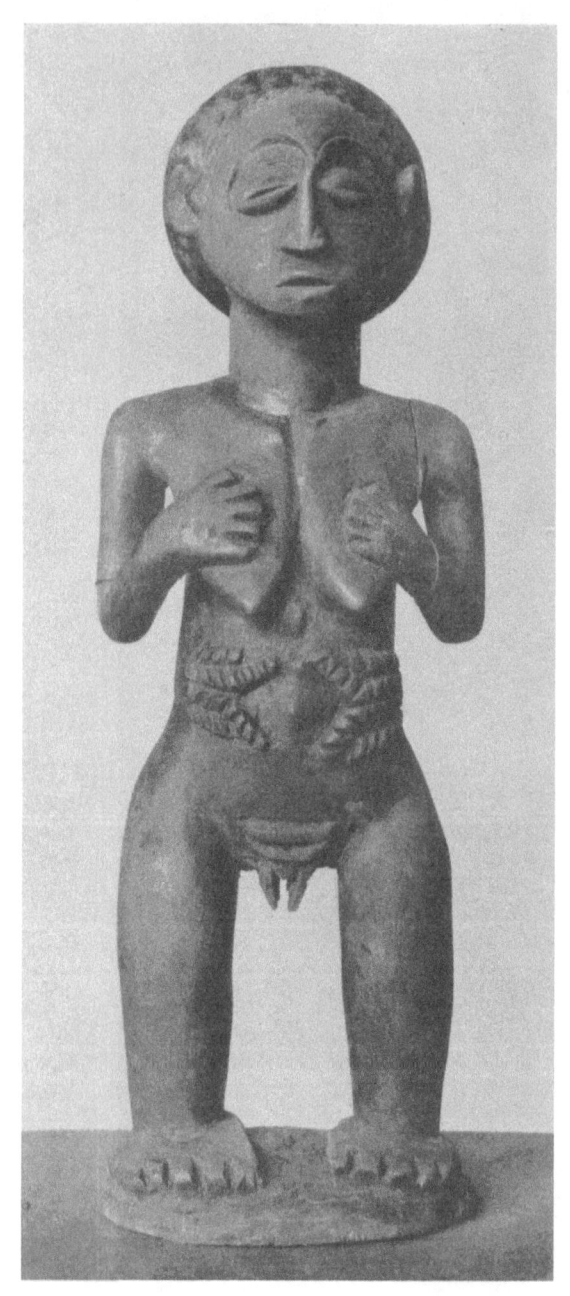

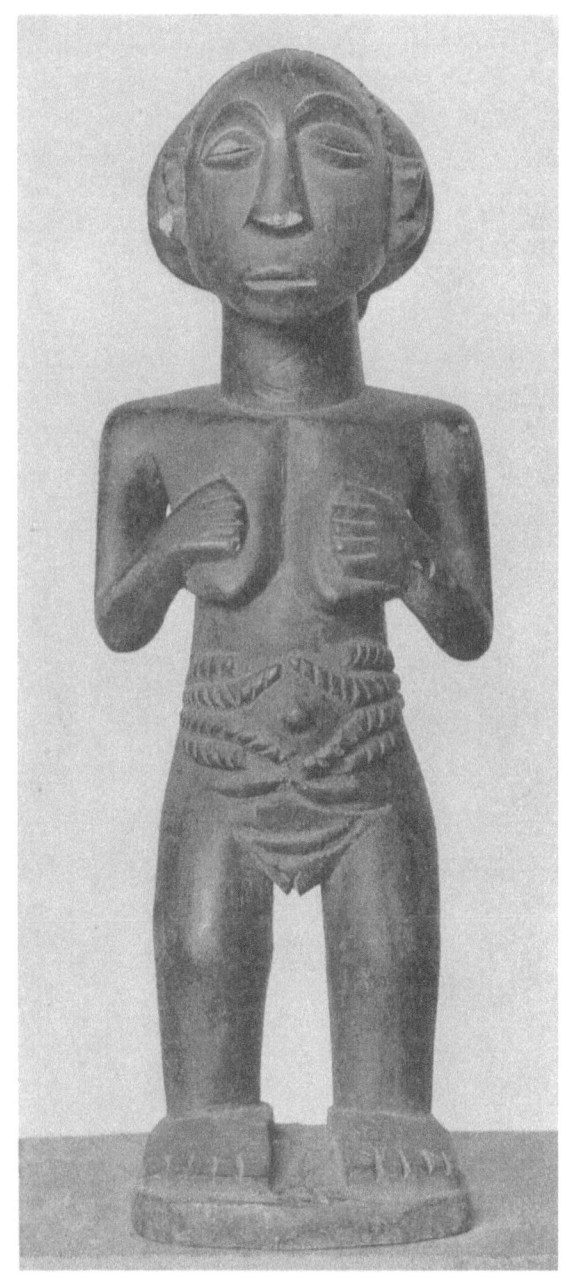

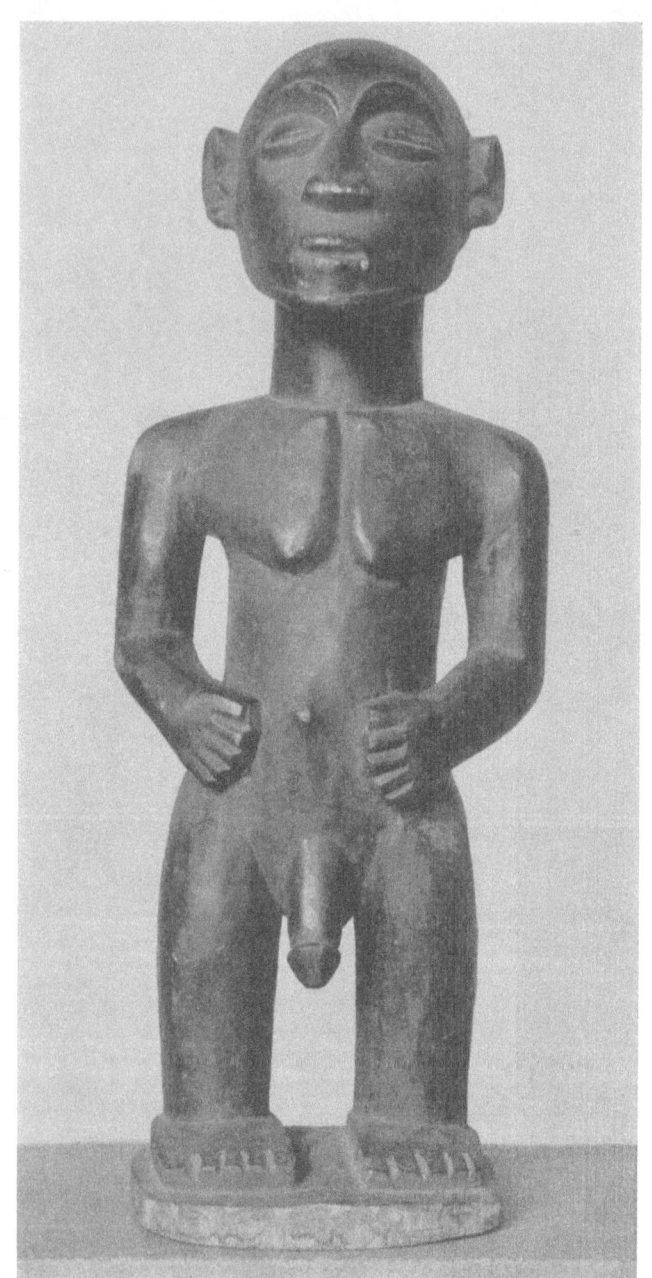

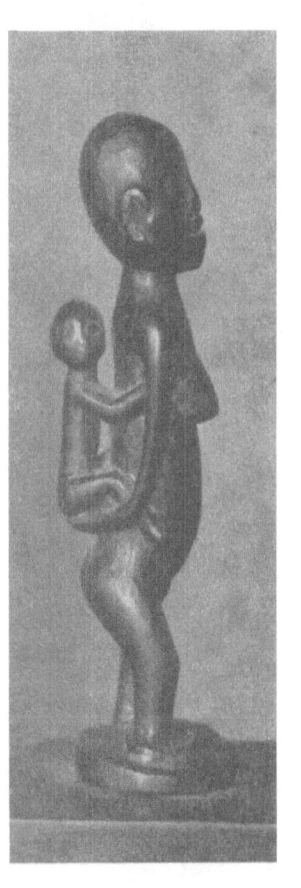 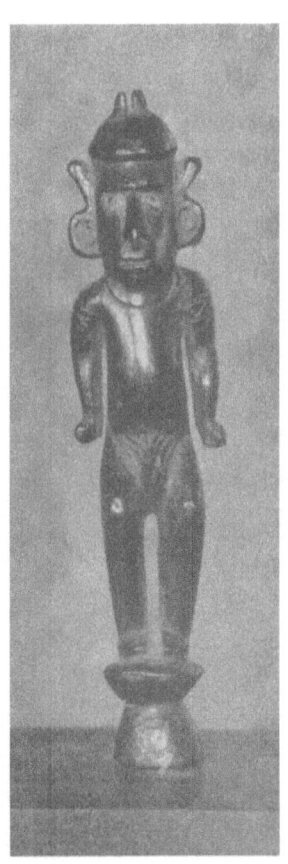

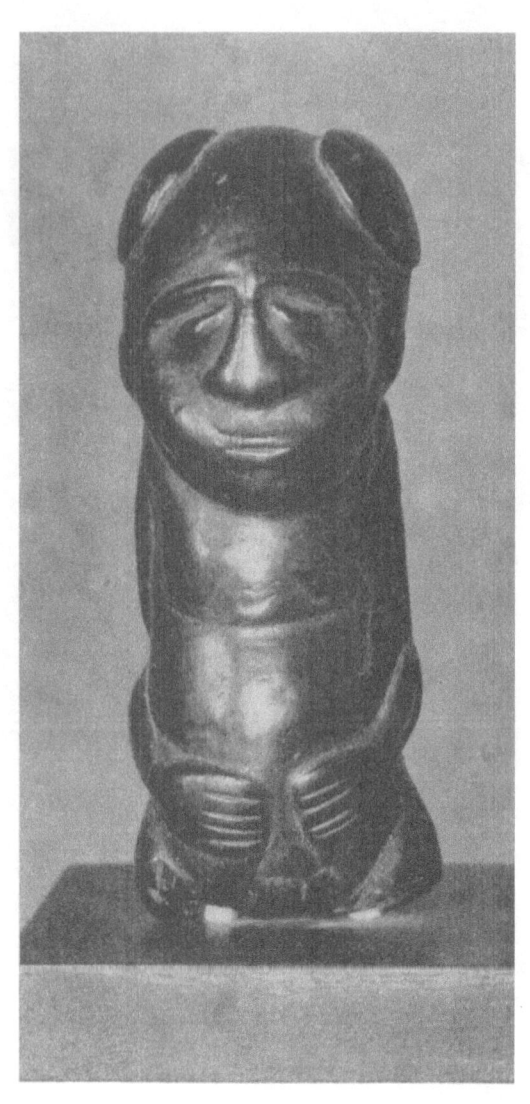

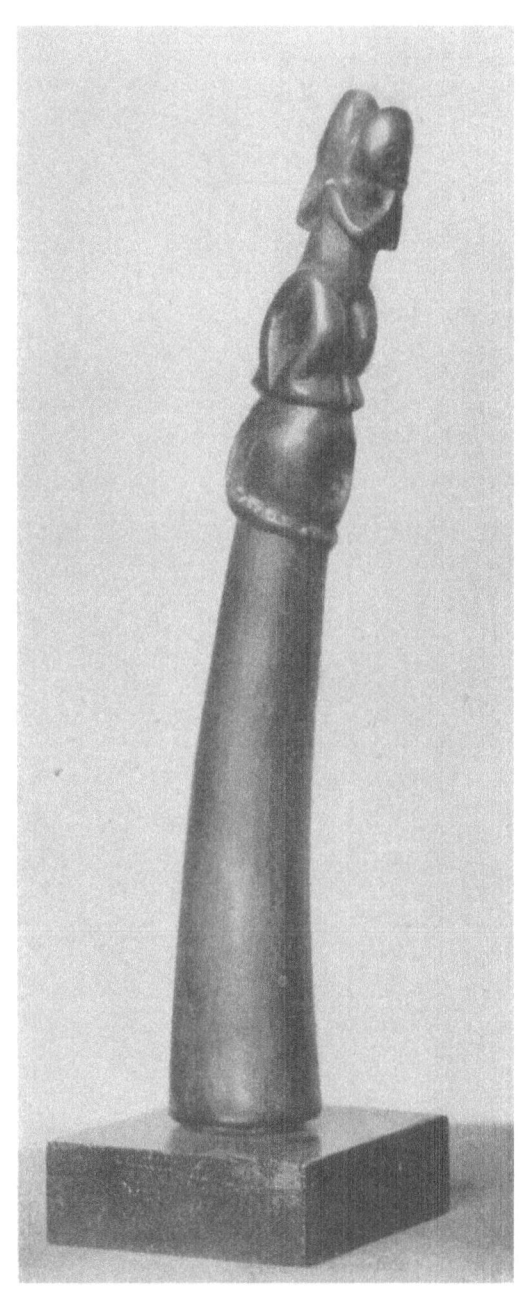

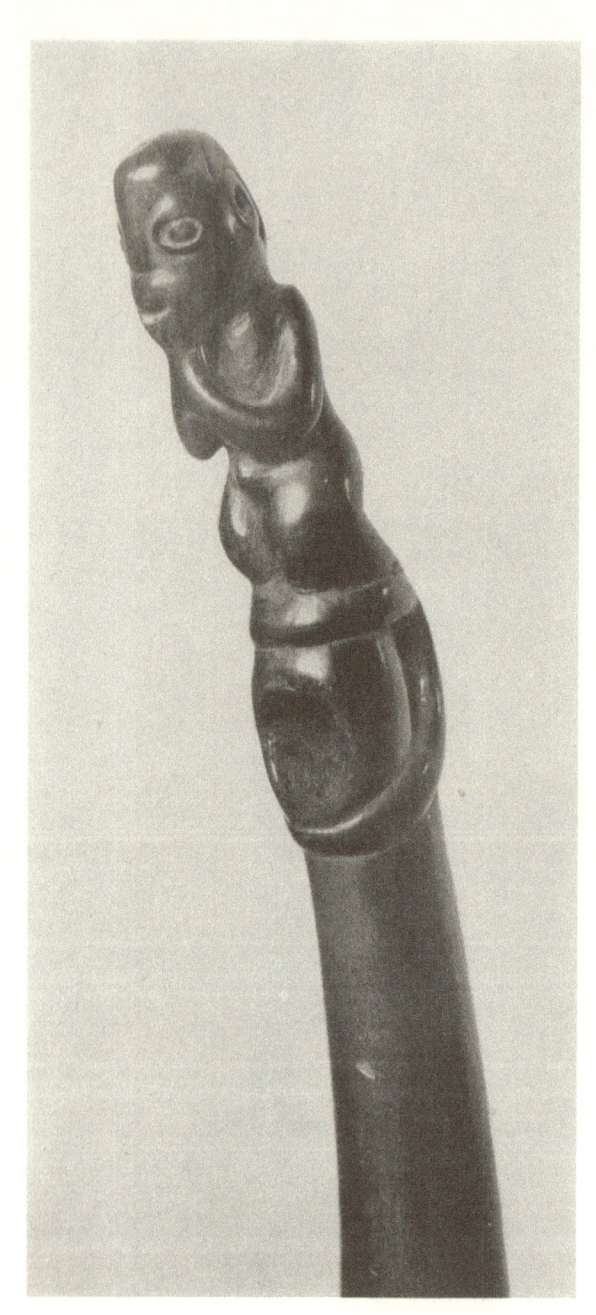

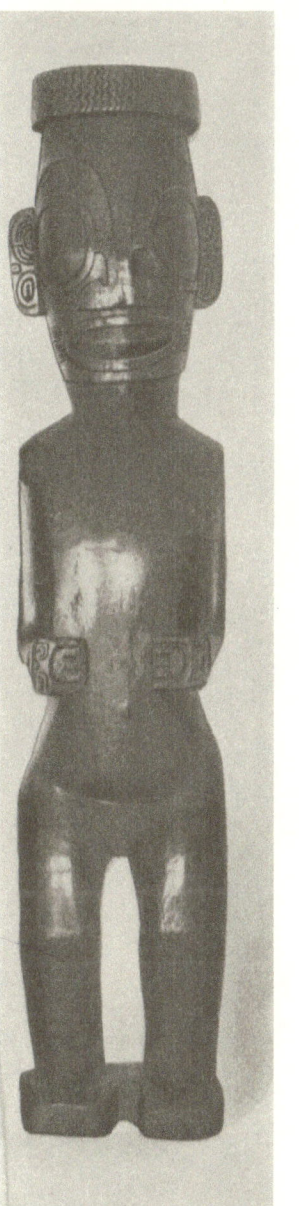
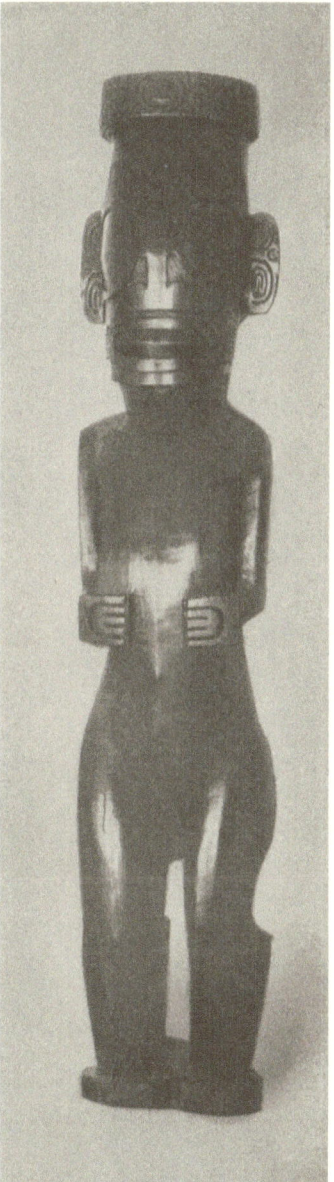

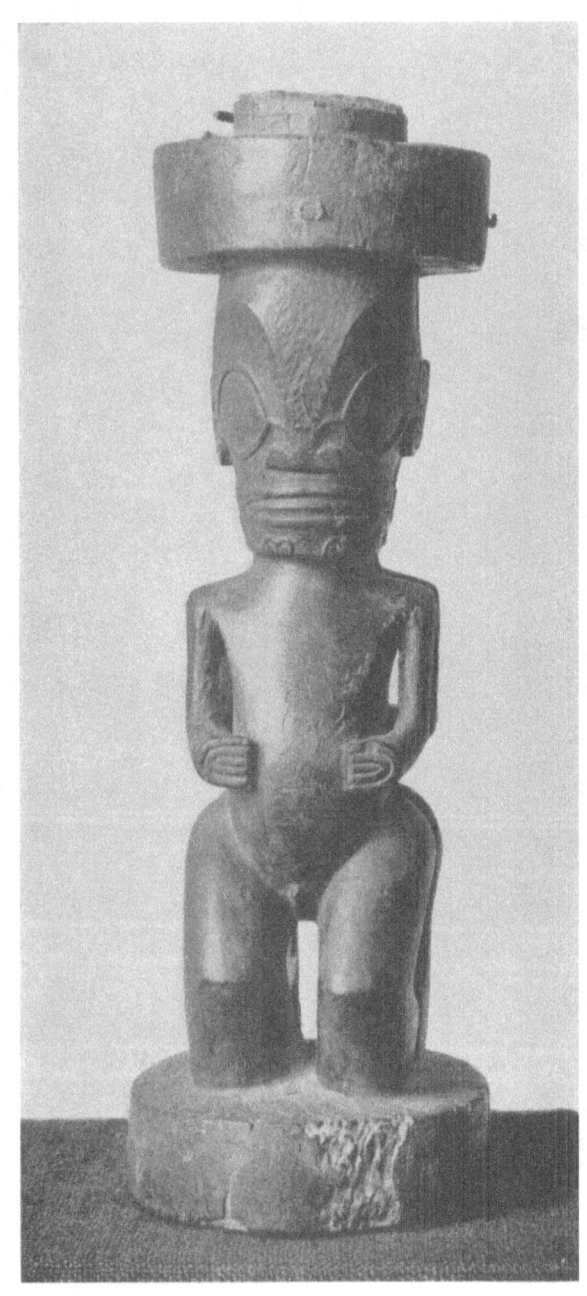

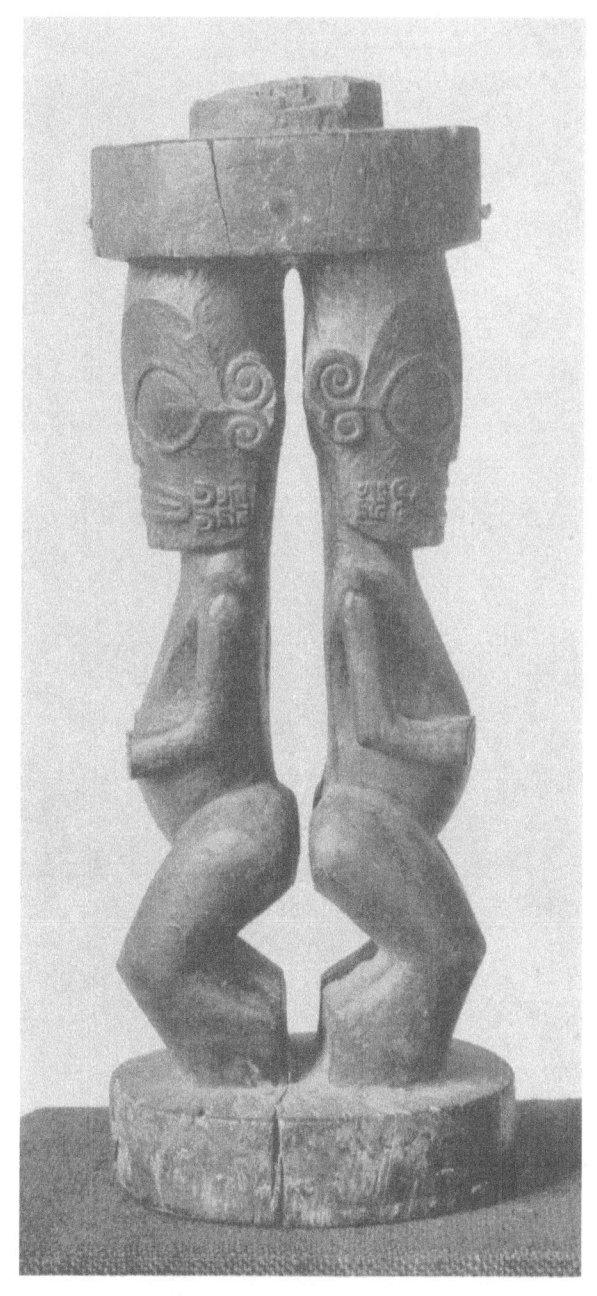

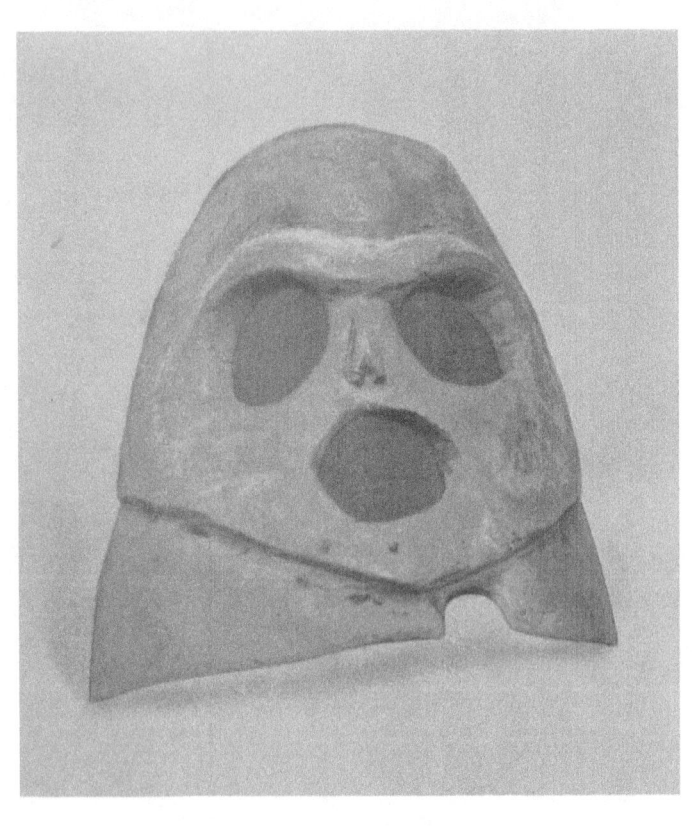

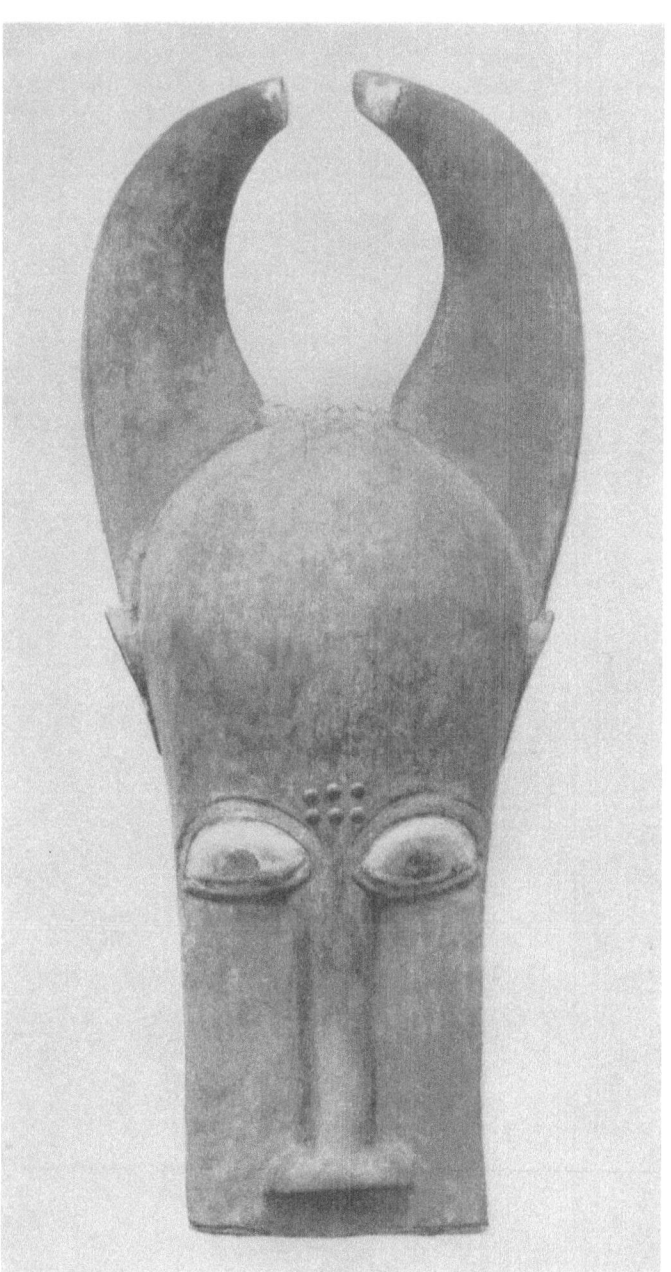

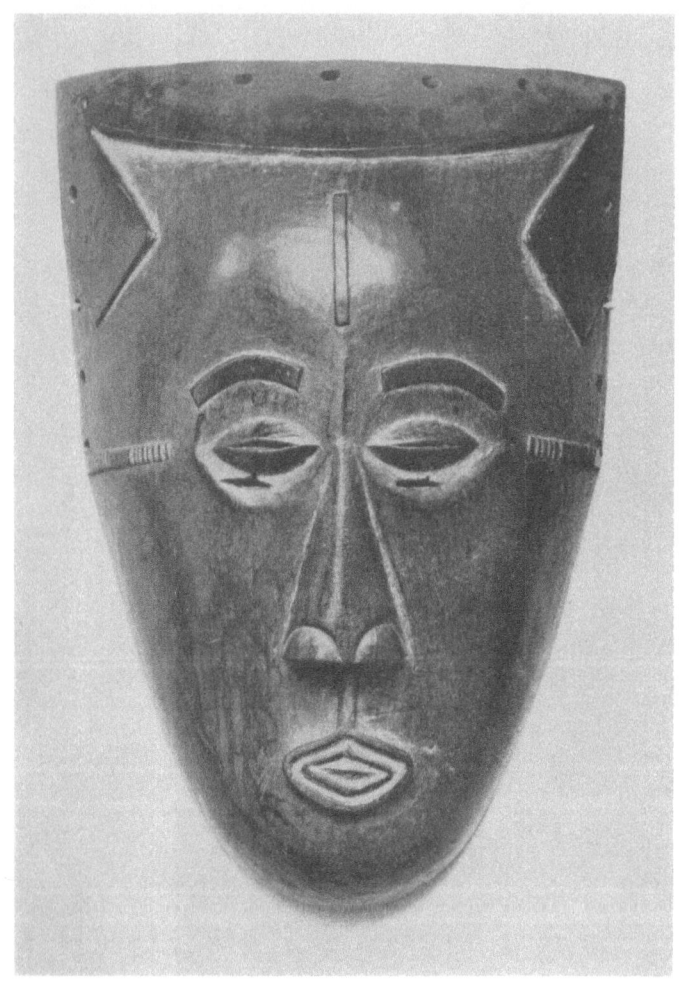

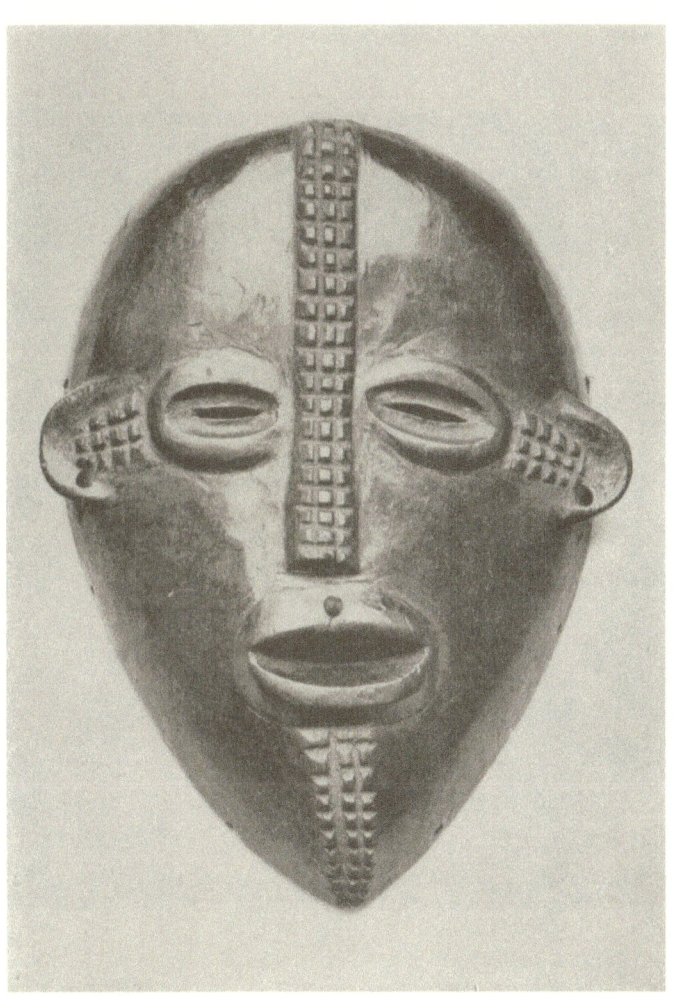

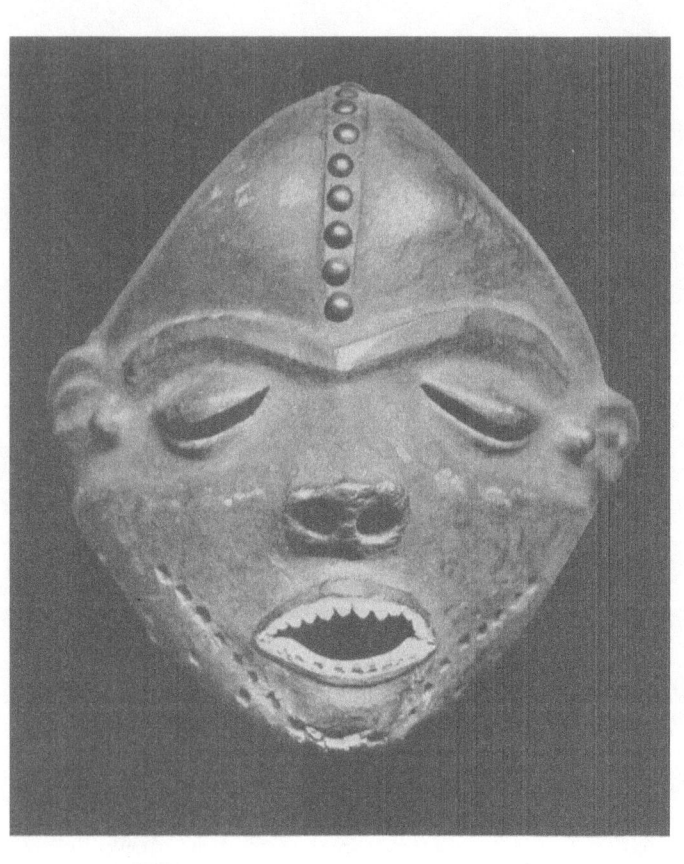

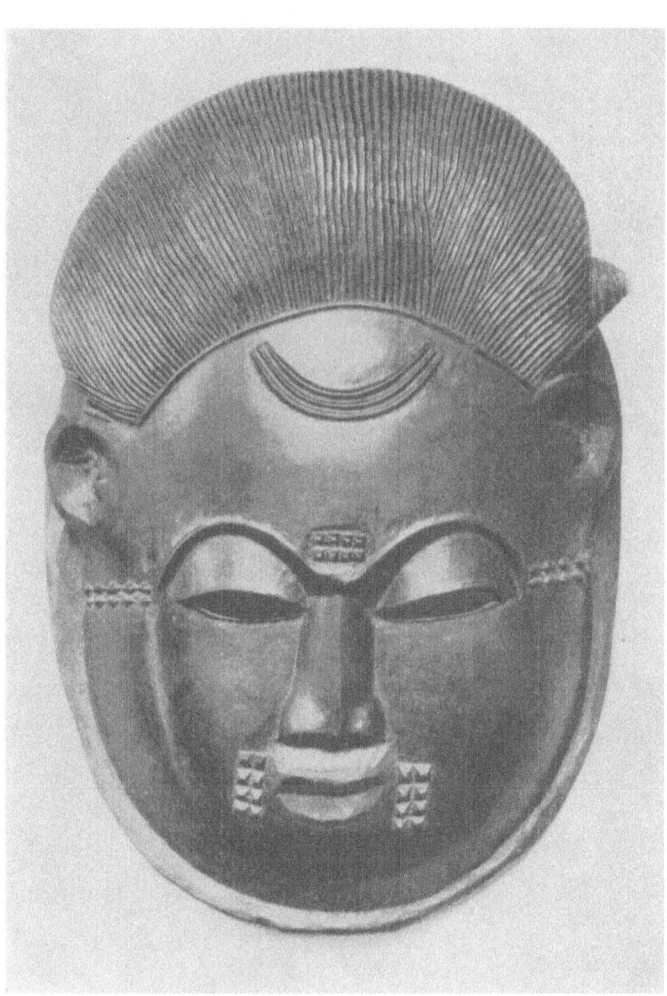

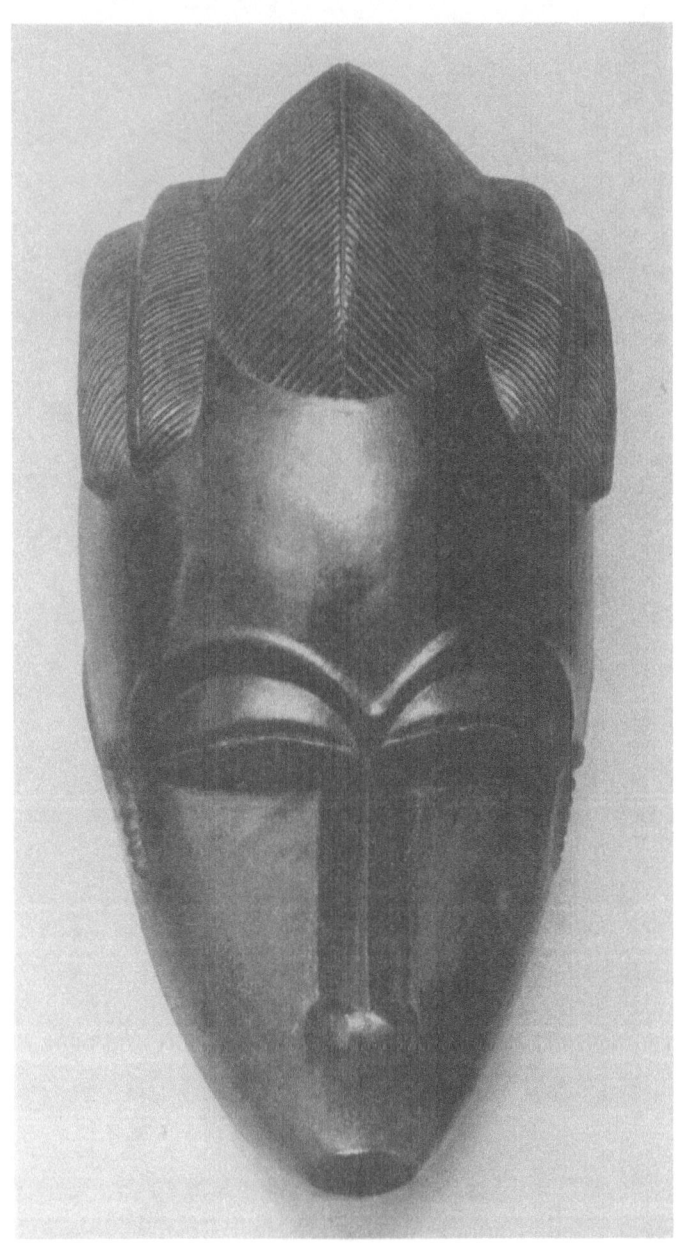

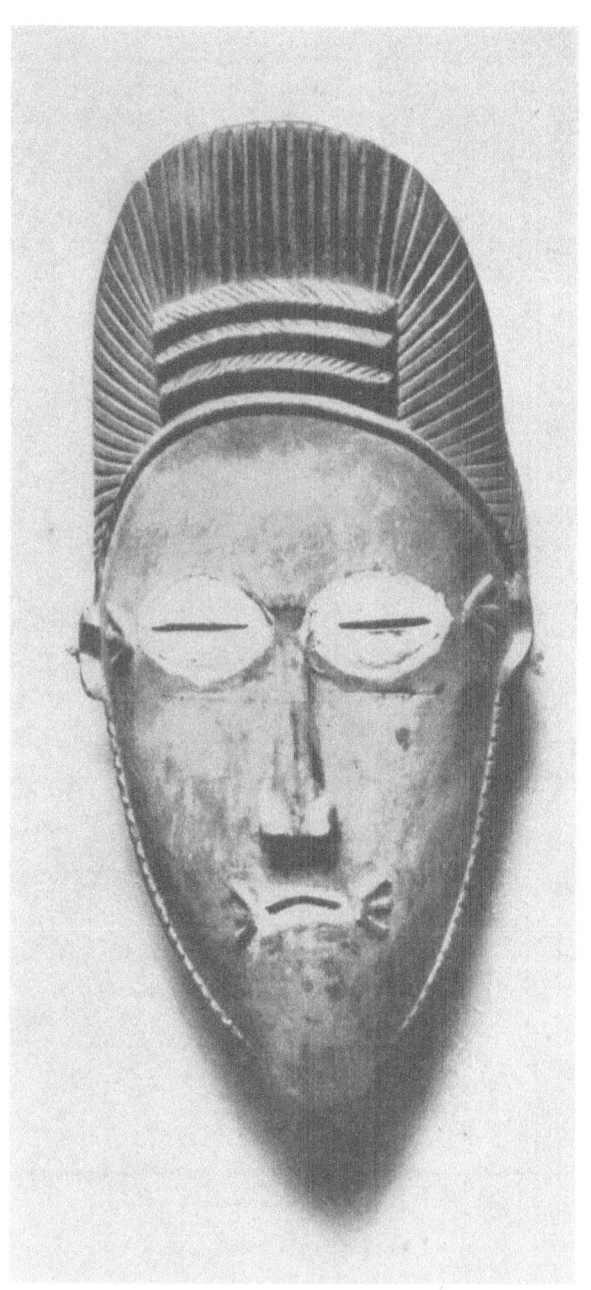

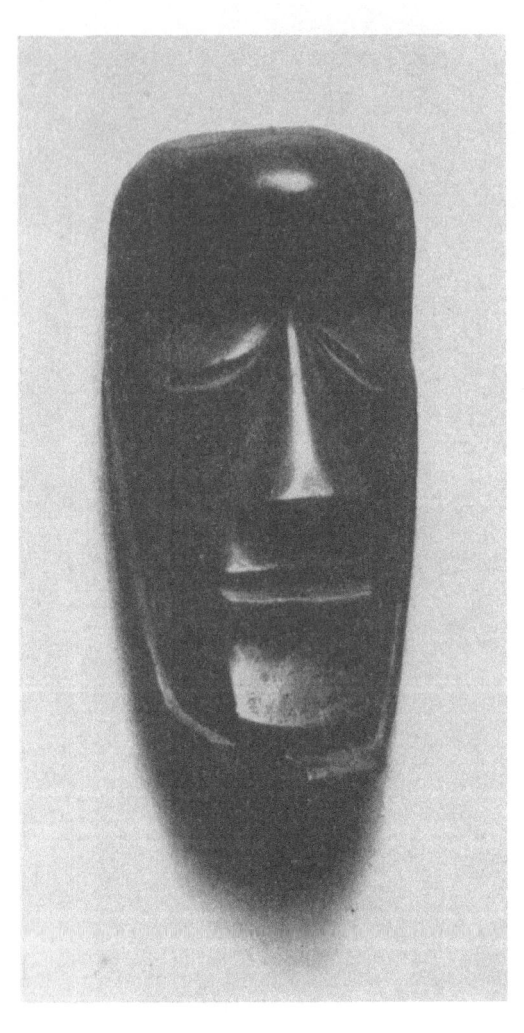

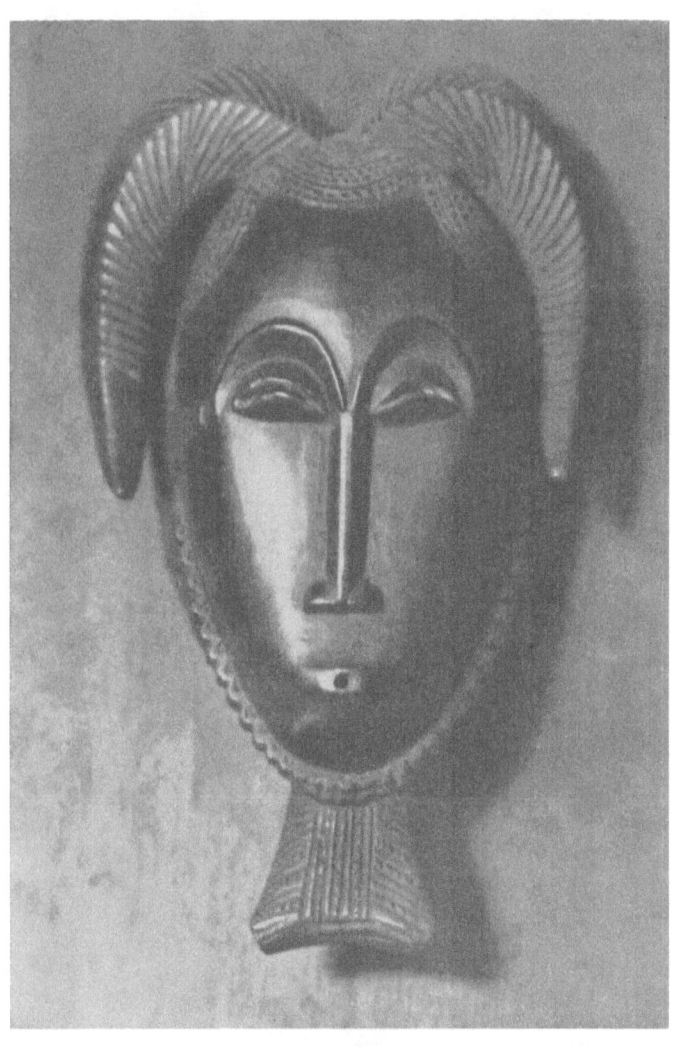

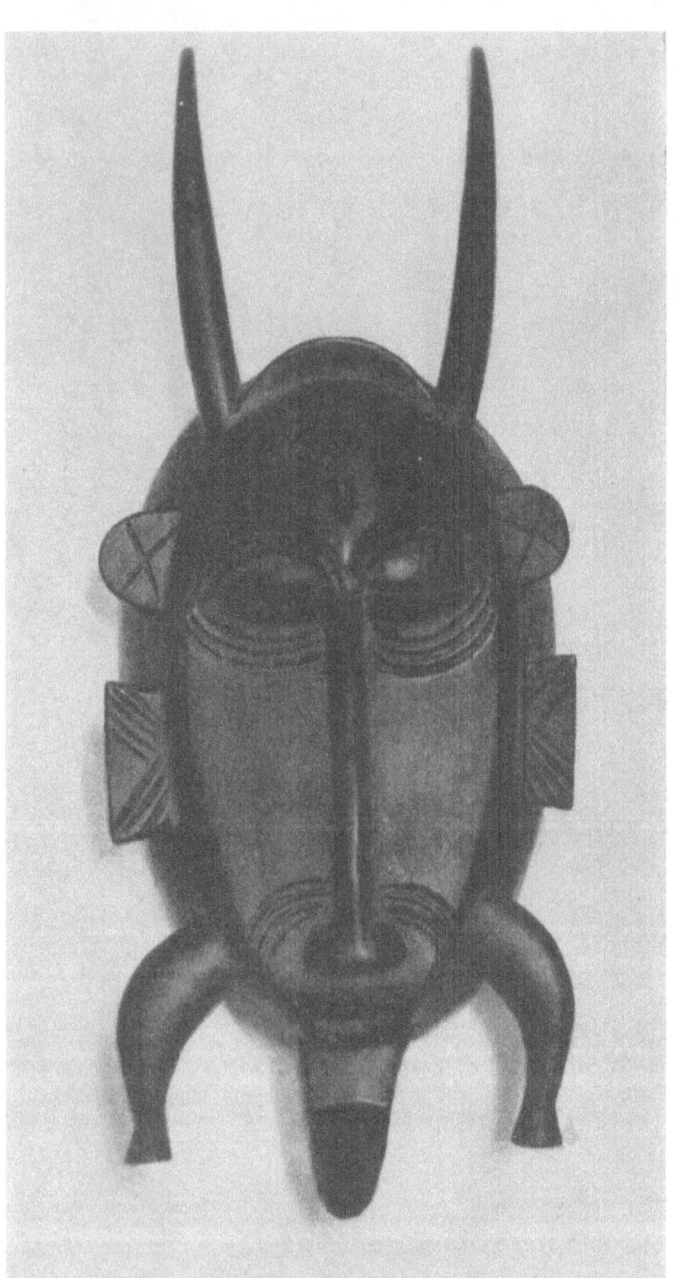

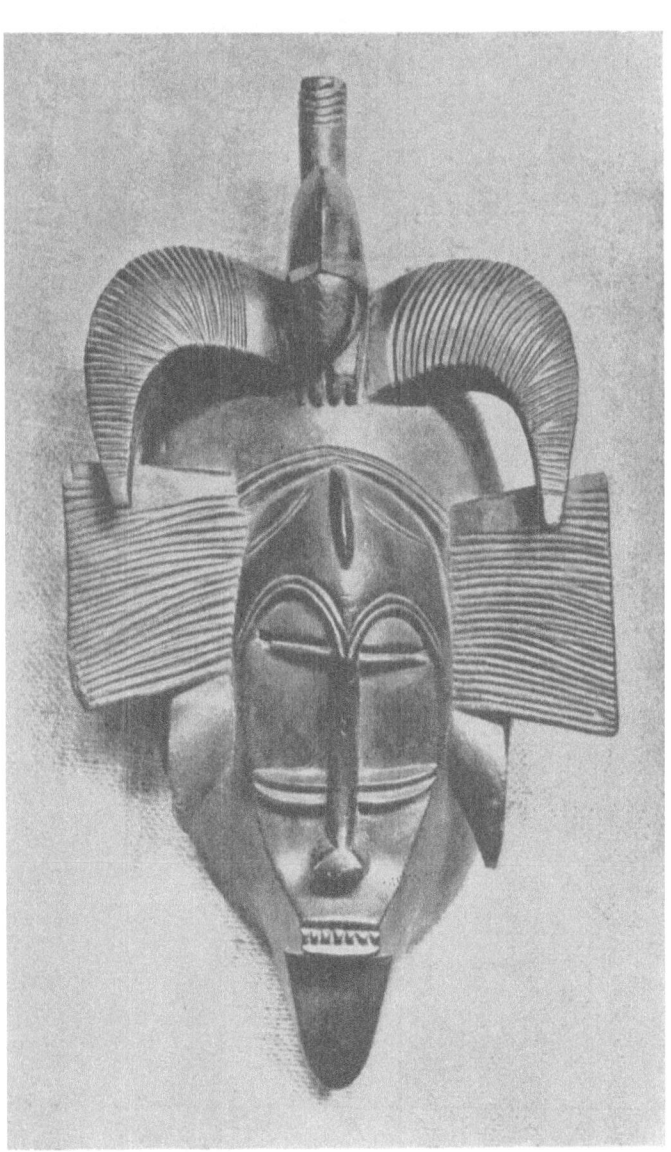

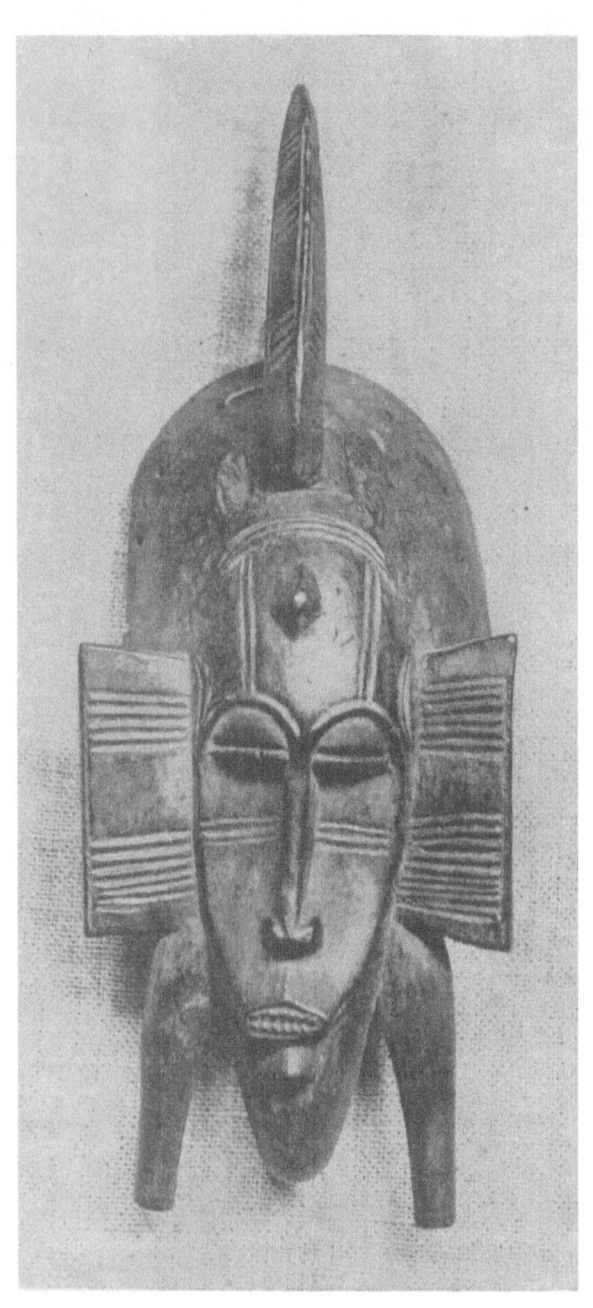

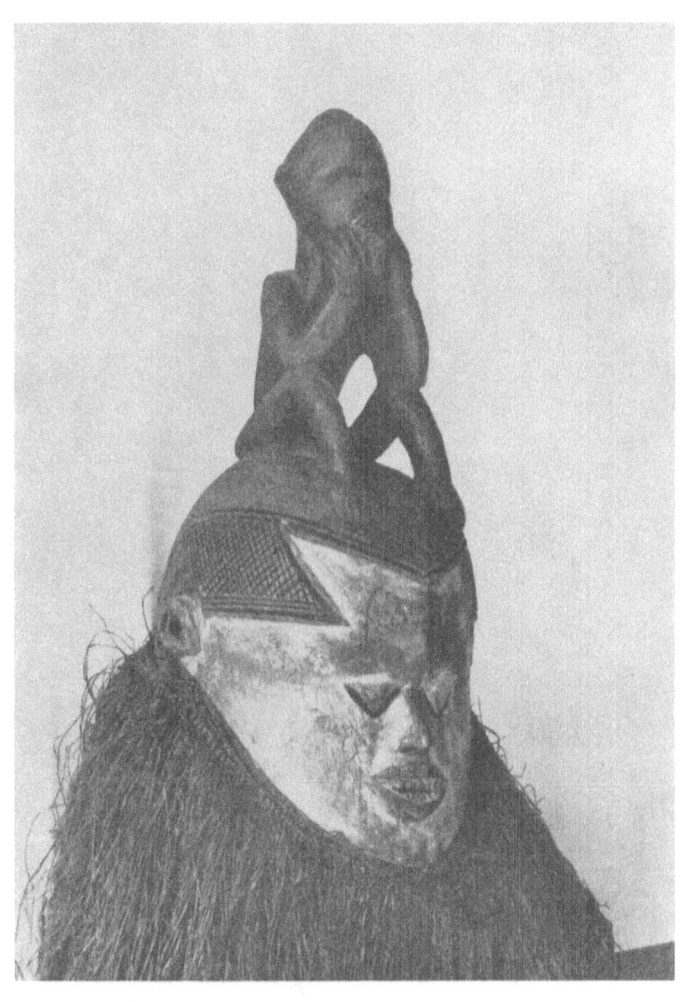

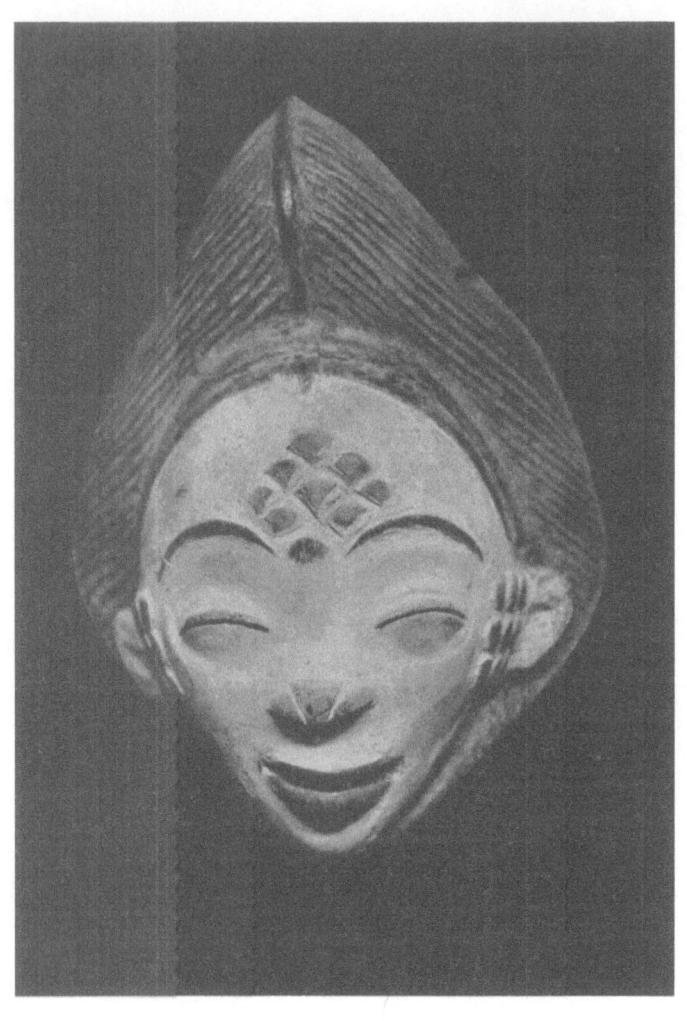

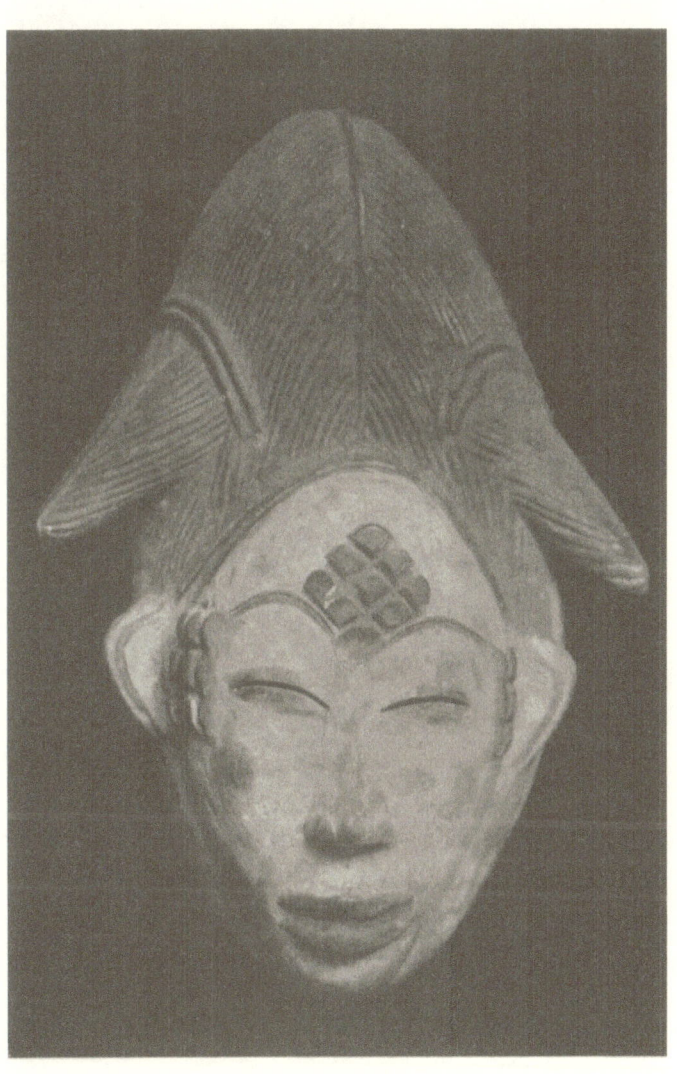

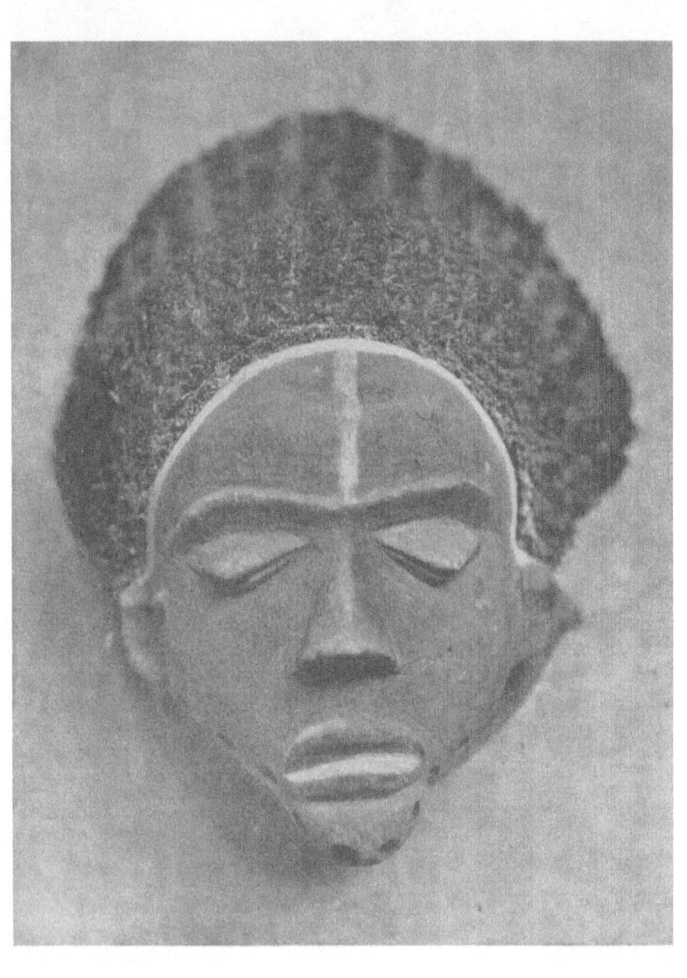

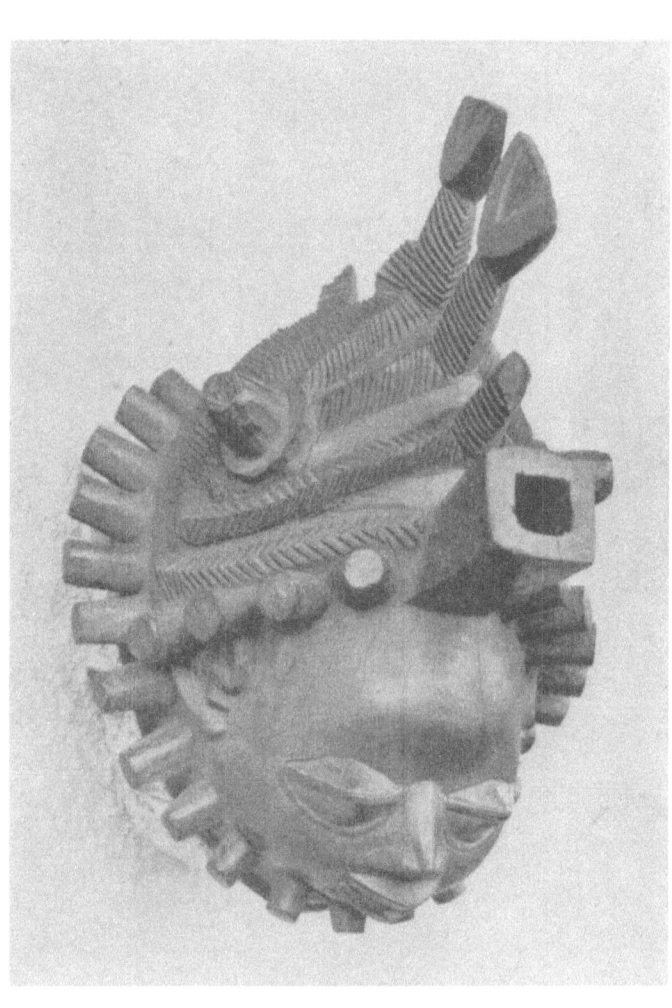

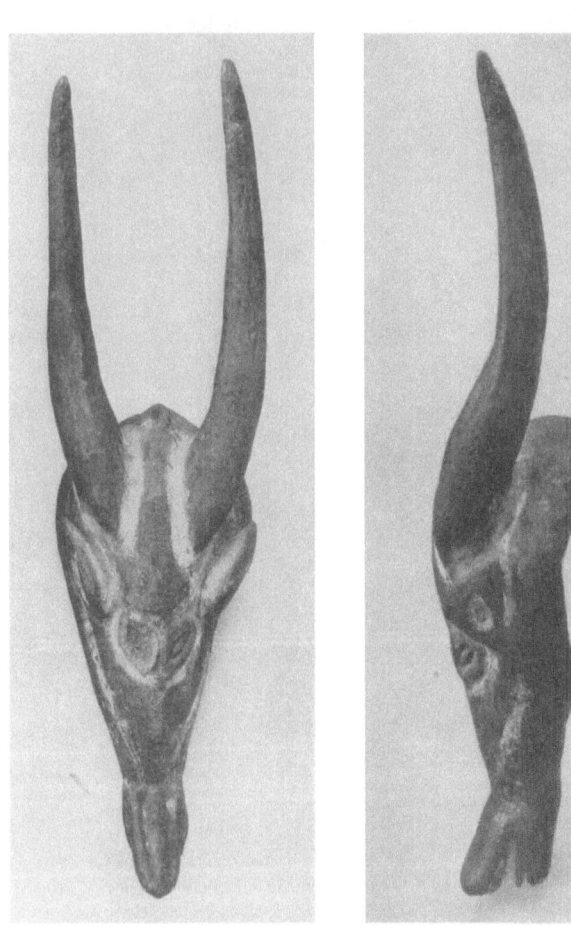

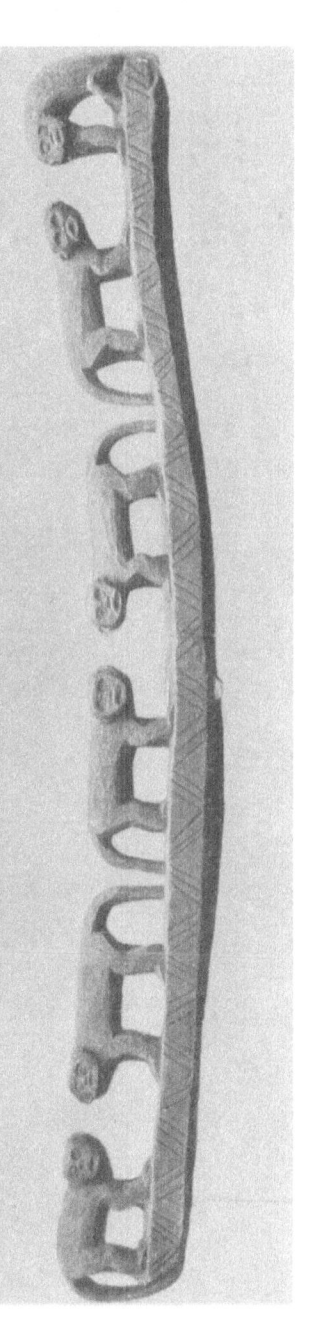

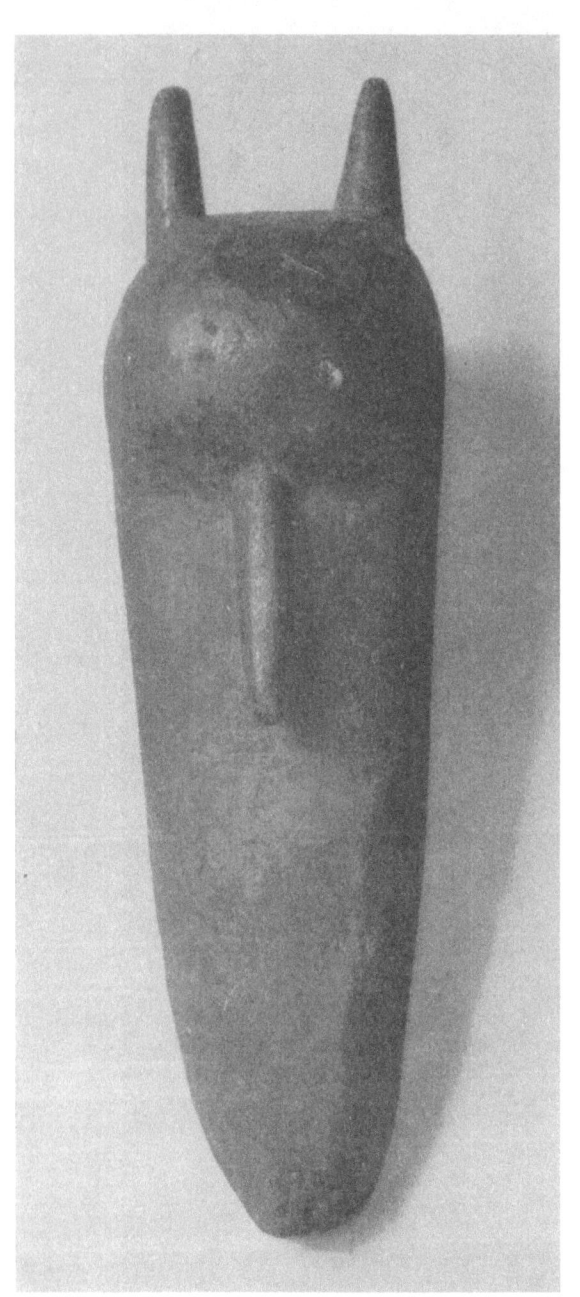

ALSO IN THIS SERIES

Karl Kraus, *In These Great Times: Selected Writings*,
translated by Patrick Healy
(ebook 2014, print forthcoming 2017).

Karl Kraus, *The Last Days of Mankind: A Tragedy in Five Acts*,
translated by Patrick Healy (print/ebook 2016).

Else Lasker-Schüler, *My Heart: A Novel of Love*,
translated by Sheldon Gilman and Robert Levine
(print/ebook 2016).

Walter Rheiner, *Cocaine: Selected Writings*,
translated by Bradley Schmidt and Gijs van Koningsveld
(ebook 2014, print forthcoming 2017).

FORTHCOMING 2017

Carl Einstein, *Bébuquin, or the dilletants of the wonder*,
translated by Patrick Healy.

Albert Ehrenstein, *Tubutsch*,
translated by Gijs van Koningsveld.

www.ingramcontent.com/pod-product-compliance
Lightning Source LLC
Chambersburg PA
CBHW031414210526
45464CB00005B/1885